WHAT TO DO WHEN YOUR CAT . . .

CHEWS ON HOUSEHOLD ITEMS, ESPECIALLY ELECTRICAL CORDS

Kittens usually need to chew on something while they're teething. Make sure yours has an appropriate chew toy and that all wiring is either hidden or sprayed with a repellent like Bitter Apple spray.

DIGS AND ELIMINATES WASTE INTO POTTED PLANTS

Digging into soil to hide urine and feces is a primal instinct for cats—but with a litter box nearby, your cat shouldn't need to do this. It may be that he doesn't like something about the litter box—check to see if you're using a new kind of kitty litter or haven't been keeping up with cleaning it.

JUMPS ON COUNTERS AND TABLETOPS

First make sure these surfaces are food and crumb-free—that's probably what's attracting your cat in the first place. If she continues to jump up, keep a spray bottle filled with water handy and immediately spray your cat while saying "No!" Putting double-sided tape on the surfaces can also be a deterrent.

**FIND OUT OTHER WAYS TO CORRECT
BOTHERSOME CAT BEHAVIORS IN
NO, KITTY!**

NO, KITTY!

A Complete A–Z
Guide for
When Your Cat
Misbehaves

STEVE DUNO

St. Martin's Paperbacks

NO, KITTY!

Copyright © 2000 by Steve Duno.
Cover photograph © Ron Kimball.

All rights reserved. No part of this book may be used or reproduced in any manner whatsoever without written permission except in the case of brief quotations embodied in critical articles or reviews. For information address St. Martin's Press, 175 Fifth Avenue, New York, NY 10010.

ISBN: 0-312-97581-3

Printed in the United States of America

St. Martin's Paperbacks edition / November 2000

10 9 8 7 6 5 4 3 2 1

CONTENTS

NO, KITTY!

INTRODUCTION

Cats are easy. Unlike the more socially demanding and emotionally needy dog, your cat can take care of himself with little help from you, save for a steady supply of food and just the right amount of attention (determined, of course, by the cat). You need not awaken at 6:00 A.M. to walk your cat or worry about leaving him home alone for a day. Cats most often come into your home house-trained and rarely require any structured obedience training. In our increasingly urbanized, space-conscious, independent society, cats now reign as the preferred pet, edging out the trusty dog in sheer numbers for over a decade now.

Owning a cat opens up a window onto the wilder ways of the world, providing something inherently seductive and longed for by those of us who sometime regret being so civilized, predictable, and contained. We envy and covet cats and keep them in our homes as companions and symbols of independence. Their grace, instincts, and demure attitudes make them less pets and more living, breathing works of art.

Unfortunately, cat ownership today is not without its pitfalls. Unlike the more malleable, pack-oriented dog, domestic cats have not changed their physiology and behavior much over the centuries, resulting in an animal with much closer ties to the wild state. Indeed, *domestic* often seems a foolish term to apply to cats, who could at any time choose to end their visit with us and return to their wild roots. Your cat's closer ties to the wild, combined with her instinctive aversion to change, make it difficult for you to modify any undesirable behaviors that might develop during your cat's life. Whereas most dogs can adopt new behaviors (or unlearn bad ones) rather easily, cats often stubbornly refuse to change their ways, making ownership of a misbehaving feline a troublesome and often frustrating experience. What's an owner to do?

Fortunately, most objectionable cat behaviors can be corrected, provided the right techniques are utilized by the owner. Highly intelligent, pragmatic, and self-centered, your cat will readily alter a behavior if he concludes that doing so will be advantageous to his lifestyle or if maintaining an unacceptable behavior become too costly or disagreeable.

That's where this book can be of use. Providing the reader with easily implemented solutions to the most common feline behavioral problems, *No, Kitty!* emphasizes *preventive* solutions whenever possible, as this is always the most effective and least traumatic way to prevent or eliminate troublesome feline misbehaviors. Unlike dogs, who respond quickly and positively to many different types of behavior modification techniques (such as leash training and vocal commands), cats often resist these methods and, due to their more sensitive natures, become traumatized by any type of negative reinforcement. Also unlike dogs, cats will hold a grudge against anyone they feel was responsible for harming or upsetting them in any way (just ask any veterinarian or cat groomer). Because of this, techniques used to correct errant feline behaviors must be well thought out and as passive as possible, with as little direct owner intervention as is feasible. *No, Kitty!* accomplishes this by first clearly showing the reader just what conditions in the cat's environment are precipitating the undesirable behavior and then clearly outlining exactly what conditions or habits he or she needs to change in the cat's life in order to end the offensive activity. In addition, the book explains *why* the cat is misbehaving, to provide owners with a better understanding of the feline psyche, in hopes that future problems might be avoided altogether.

When simple modifications to the cat's environment are not enough to reduce or eliminate an offensive feline behavior, *No, Kitty!* provides the reader with behavior modification techniques tailored to the feline mind, designed to be as benign and effective as possible. Distraction and desensitization techniques are used, as are passive discouragement methods (such as placing clear strips of double-sided sticky tape around areas or objects off-limits to the cat) and, when necessary, mildly unpleasant procedures such as a quick squirt from a water pistol. Under no circumstances are any harmful, humiliating, disrespectful, or frightening methods used to stop an undesirable feline behavior, so as to preserve not only your cat's dignity, safety, and peace of mind but also her respect and affection for her owner.

In addition to offering the reader workable solutions to the most common cat problems, *No, Kitty!*

provides him or her with an invaluable primer on basic feline needs, desires, and instincts and also lists the "Ten Commandments" of cat ownership, rules that every owner should abide by when interacting with his or her pet in order to maintain a mutually beneficial, respectful relationship. Altogether, the reader gets a complete package, one that is sure to make cat ownership a much more enjoyable experience.

My motivations for writing this problem-solving book were twofold. First, I want to make cat ownership as pleasant and rewarding as possible for you and your cat. Neither you nor your pet will long tolerate a stress-filled, mutually antagonistic relationship. Unfortunately for the cat, when push comes to shove it's the misbehaving cat who will ultimately go and not the owner. These delinquent felines rarely find new homes and very often wind up in a local animal shelter, where they will ultimately be euthanized, if not quickly adopted by a tolerant benefactor willing to spend some time modifying the cat's improper behavior. The sad truth is that many thousands of cats are put to sleep in this country either because no one wants them or no one has the time or motivation to retrain them to be good housemates. It is my hope that this book will help lessen this terrible toll.

The second motivation I have for writing this book is simple: I want to show readers just how smart and malleable cats really can be. The notion that they are intractable and intellectually rigid is not true. They simply learn differently than dogs do and are motivated by more, shall we say, narcissistic stimuli. As they have always been for the most part loners, cats have never quite mastered the complexities of "pack" living and thus do not have the same learning motivators in place that canines do. No matter; we will simply turn to training methods that the solitary, crafty, self-aware feline can understand.

The bottom line is that your cat can be taught to behave, or to stop misbehaving, provided you have the time and inclination to help him see the light.

PART ONE

The Cat: What You Need to Know First

Cats are survivors, and masters of accommodation. Existing in nearly every climactic zone the planet has to offer, these efficient, elegant animals have thrived many millions of years longer than us humans and will most likely be cavorting about years after we are gone. Leave your ten-pound domestic dog alone in the middle of the wilderness, and he will probably become coyote food within a week; do the same with your cat, and he will most likely be hunting down and eating chipmunks before the first day has passed. Independent, self-sufficient, and proud, today's feline is a beautiful, capable realist, a companion more than a pet. It is no wonder millions of us have readily chosen to share our lives with one.

THE CAT'S BASIC DRIVES

Cats owe their success to a wonderfully designed body, a keen, adaptive mind, and a set of strong instincts, or drives. To begin to understand your cat's behavior, you must first comprehend what motivates him to do the things he does. What are your cat's priorities? What basic drives are present, and how do they affect the animal's day-to-day behavior and his interactions with you? Developing a better understanding of your cat's instinctual needs and desires will open a window to the feline psyche for you, letting you see the reasons and motivations behind his actions, be they desirable or not.

Food

Eating is an essential, age-old drive for all animals, particularly the cat. Along with the drive to reproduce, the drive to find and consume food has been and continues to be the strongest motivator in the animal kingdom. From the microscopic amoeba right up to our own species, to eat is to live.

Of the world's predators, few can confess to being as successful as the cat. Blessed with large brains, athletic bodies, and the superb ability to quietly stalk prey, cats both in the wild and in domesticity are more than a match for the unsuspecting animal unlucky enough to be called dinner. Obtaining food is a very serious and elemental drive, not only for the wild cats but for your pet as well. Domesticity has not dulled your feline friend's ability to hunt or her desire to eat. Recognize this, and you will be able to understand many aspects of your cat's everyday behavior, such as her desire to get into your parakeet's cage or your guppy's bowl.

Though your cat has no real need to hunt for food, her instinct to do so is still intact. If you have any doubts about this, simply observe the behavior of six-week-old littermates. They relish the chance to stalk each other, and will pounce on any moving toy that comes into their sight. Those of you who allow your felines access to the outdoors probably have been blessed with occasional "gifts," small, unlucky rodents or birds casually dropped at your doorstep by your resident predator, proud trophies that reveal just how capable your cat remains.

Your cat's predatory or food drive is one of his strongest drives. Evidence of this can readily be seen around feeding time. Though usually not as ravenous as the family dog, your cat will most likely savor his moments around the food dish and may greedily defend it, showing varying signs of aggression when another pet comes too close to the bounty. This behavior can be especially common when a new cat is introduced into an established cat's domain and tries to weasel up to the food dish while the older cat is eating. This type of behavior, though unpleasant, is not necessarily abnormal and should not surprise an owner who attempts to introduce a new feline into the older cat's home. Few adult cats, save lions and cheetahs in the wild, have much of a history of sharing food with others of their species except their young. Instead, they hunt and feed alone.

Your cat shares this instinct. The only time in domestic cats' lives that they tolerate sharing food is during kittenhood, when they must put up with several other hungry mouths around them. That tolerance is a survival tool that gradually fades away as the cat matures. Domestic cats who have been neutered at a reasonably early age do tend to be more tolerant of sharing food with other cats, however, due to the "kittenish" mentality that neutering can foster in an otherwise physically mature animal.

Because eating is such a strong drive for your cat, you will be able to utilize it to help shape or change her behavior. After all, you are the provider of that food and as such can use it to reinforce desirable behaviors or discourage undesirable ones. Most cats, if fed on a predictable schedule, will respond quite well to food offerings and will quickly learn whatever behavior is desired of them in exchange for a tasty tidbit.

Territory

In the wild, most cats are solitary hunters who stake out a distinct hunting territory, then jealously defend it from all other cats. The reason for doing so is clear and twofold. First, in order for predators such as cats to survive, they must be assured of an adequate supply of prey. In order to achieve that, each cat must lay claim to a territory large enough to hold a big-enough population of prey animals to support the cat. Any smaller and the cat in question would not be able to survive and would instead have to invade the territory of another animal, a risky, life-threatening venture. A careful balance develops, then, between competing cats in the wild. Territorial boundaries are marked through the spaying of urine, defecating, and making scratch marks on trees. Through fear and respect these solitary feline hunters maintain an uneasy understanding with neighboring competitors.

The other reason that cats in the wild try to maintain a distinct territory is to ensure that a high-enough number of mates will be available. This is generally a concern of the males, who must have within their territories a sufficient number of females to breed with. The larger the territory, the greater the opportunity to mate. Older or weaker males not able to maintain a large-enough territory will not pass their genes along to future generations. Their lines will run out, in favor of those of the stronger, more territorial cats.

The interesting factor in territorial drive is not the size of the territory, however, but the availability of prey. In situations where the density of prey animals is very high, territories can be quite small. For example, stray cats living near a garbage dump might number in the hundreds, due to the ready supply of food. These cats become less solitary, readily tolerating the presence of other felines because of the abundance of food. Why fight and risk injury when there is enough for all? So, when food is plentiful, cats become less solitary and more tolerant of each other.

Recognizing your cat's territorial drive will help foster a safer, happier environment for him and for yourself. For example, being aware of your cat's territorial instincts will, I hope, deter you from impulsively bringing home three abandoned rottweiler puppies, two guinea pigs, and an eight-year-old alley cat!

Your cat will try to claim his territory by marking, scratching, or fighting with other animals who try to invade his space. Though these behaviors are predictable, they are not acceptable inside your home. How to deal with them is covered in detail later in this book. The territorial drive can be minimized somewhat, however, by raising your cat with another of his kind or even with a puppy and by making sure that food never becomes an issue of contention. A well-fed cat, after all, will be a much less contentious one.

Safety

All cats want to live in a safe, secure environment. None of them enjoy unexpected events or changes in the normal flow of things. They want their everyday lives to be as predictable as possible. You may have noticed that your cat does not always react well to strangers or to unscheduled events, such as a vigorous rap on the door or the neighbor dropping by with her three young children. He may disappear for hours at a time, or until the strange intruders have gone home. The reason for this is simple: a cat won't feel safe unless his environment is familiar and nonthreatening. In order to help prevent abnormal behaviors from surfacing in your cat, you will need to be aware of his need to feel comfortable and in control. Avoiding too many unexpected guests, deafening music, and constant changes in the home environment will help keep your cat happy and problem-free.

Sex

The drive to mate and produce offspring is a strong one in all unneutered cats. By the time a male or female cat is seven months old, he or she will begin to show a desire to do so. For those owners who have not had their cats neutered, this drive can cause a number of unwanted behaviors. Males will want to go outside and roam; in doing so, they will get into fights with other males, possibly getting injured in the process. If limited to the home environment, the unneutered male will most likely mark all over the house and become very vocal in an attempt to voice his desire to go outside and find a female. Unneutered females allowed to go outdoors will ultimately become pregnant, repeatedly, and may also get into fights, with males and females. If kept indoors, the unneutered female will become extremely vocal and possibly mark or spot all over the house.

Fortunately, unwanted behavior due to the cat's sex drive can be easily dealt with by having your cat neutered by his or her sixth or seventh month. Castration for the male and spaying for the female will quickly quell most of these unwanted behaviors. Unless your cat is a prized purebreed, there really is no need to put off neutering. In addition to putting a halt to the aforementioned unwanted behaviors, neutering will help extend the life of your pet, preventing several types of cancer and minimizing the chance of the cat getting into a life-threatening fight with a bigger, meaner animal. In addition, having your cat neutered will help prevent one of the domestic cat's most pressing problems: rampant overpopulation. One visit to your local animal shelter will be all you'll need to convince yourself. When faced with a litter of unwanted kittens, many owners simply take the poor babies to the nearest shelter, thinking that they will be adopted quickly. Unfortunately, the supply far exceeds the demand, causing tens of thousands of kittens in this country alone to be euthanized each year. Neutering your cat, perhaps more than any other act, will prevent many unwanted behavior problems and help put a halt to the ceaseless, unnecessary killing of innocent kittens.

Parenting

The urge to care for the young is a strong drive in female cats, as it is in all mammals. The desire to be loved and cared for is also strong, particularly among kittens, who crave the company and attention of their mother and littermates. Being aware of these drives will help you understand your cat better, in a number of ways. First, if your cat is a nursing mother, you will know to respect her space, especially when she is with her kittens. Keeping strangers and rambunctious children away from her while she is interacting with her litter will help prevent unnecessary aggression and will allow the kittens to receive the motherly attentions they need to mature properly.

Cats socialize with their own kind more during kittenhood than at any other time. This short eight-to-ten-week period of intense play and companionship with littermates is vital to kittens, because it teaches them all about feline manners and helps to minimize fear-aggressive tendencies later in life. Kittens not allowed to interact with their mothers and littermates through at least the seventh or eight week of life will often become antisocial adults, who cannot stand the company of other cats and who will in all likelihood shun the attentions of most humans, save their owners. Kittens also need to interact with their mothers and other kittens in order to develop a need for sibling and maternal attentions, a need usually transferred to the kitten's new human owner. Kittens who learn to love their mothers and respect their littermates will carry that love to their new homes. This phenomenon explains how our cats think about us. We are not so much leaders or owners to them but rather mother figures or littermates. Many domestic cats in this way remain somewhat childlike throughout their lives, at least when interacting with us. In comparison, cats in the wild mature quickly and almost always cut off all contact with siblings or parents once out on their own.

If you have a cat who shows profound fear aggression toward guests, other cats, or even yourself, odds are he was taken from his litter too soon and not allowed to learn how to interact properly. For this reason, you should never take kittens from their mothers and littermates until they are at least eight weeks old.

Play

Yes, playing is a normal drive in cats, especially for kittens and adolescent cats. In kittens it is a vital activity, helping them develop motor skills and stalking abilities and socializing them so they can properly interact with others of their own kind. Play is essential to a kitten's psychological and physiological development, as it is with all mammal babies.

During play kittens learn all about the dominance hierarchy in the litter. Though not as pronounced in cats as in dogs, a pecking order does exist for them. They need to discover where they fit in the scheme of things. Are they near the top of the litter or closer to the bottom? Being allowed to work this out through games of strength and possession is crucial to a cat's future sense of self and to developing tolerance of other cats.

Through play, cats learn to groom themselves. By observing their mothers' and their littermates' actions, kittens will begin to playfully groom each other in an attempt to mimic the behavior. This teaches them proper kitty hygiene and helps teach them to tolerate being handled and groomed later in life.

The drive to play also serves a crucial purpose for the mother, particularly among wild cats. As the mother is forced to regularly leave her kittens to hunt for food, her litter with their playful antics serve as a good "baby-sitter" of sorts for one another, keeping the kittens busy while she is gone. Through play, the litter stays together until she comes back home with dinner.

Last, the play instinct helps kittens to learn about their immediate environment. During play, kittens will often explore their surroundings, a behavior that helps feed the cat's insatiable curiosity and teaches them valuable lessons about safety.

By the time a cat is four or five months old, the drive to play begins to level off, then wane. The adult cat's penchant for individuality begins to set in; other cats, instead of being seen as playmates, become rivals, adversaries, or potential mates. If allowed to stay with their respective litters for the first eight weeks, though, most cats will retain much of that playful mentality, directing it toward you instead of others of their own kind.

Curiosity

Most cats have an instinctive need to explore or investigate, as do all intelligent creatures. Scrutinizing every little thing that comes into the line of sight is a natural reaction for any hunter. Through this instinct cats learn about their world and develop their intellect. Denied a stimulating environment, most cats will become antisocial, lethargic, and possibly destructive. You should always provide your cat with interesting, mentally stimulating things to see and do, to ensure that he remains happy and healthy.

Rest

All cats tend to spend more time sleeping each day than they do being awake. An adult cat might spend as many as fourteen hours or more each day curled up in a sleepy ball on your sofa or bed, dreaming of chasing mice or sparrows in the backyard. Though the reason for so much sleep is unclear, researchers believe that kittens' brains develop most during sleep, necessitating the long periods of inactivity. In addition, most cats are quite active and alert while awake, perhaps requiring them to get more sleep than many other mammals.

Acknowledging and understanding these basic feline drives will go a long way in helping you relate to your cat. You will be able to anticipate a larger number of his behaviors more easily and discern in advance just what his reaction to an up coming situation will be. That is one of the goals of this book: if you can predict an undesirable behavior before it occurs, you can head it off at the pass. For instance, by knowing that a cat prefers stability in its environment you might decide against adopting those three adorable basset hound puppies you saw at the shelter. Or, now being aware of your cat's covetousness toward his food, you might decide that allowing your two-year-old child to stick her face into your cat's dish while he eats is probably a bad idea. Remember, prevention is preferable to behavior modification every time.

THE MARVELOUS FELINE ANATOMY

The cat is an incredible physical specimen. Throughout history we have been amazed by cats' physical abilities, which set them apart from most other domestic pets and helped create the legendary mystique surrounding all felines.

The cat's physical attributes are almost too numerous to list. Cats are supremely quiet when moving. They have unparalleled balance, can leap up, down, or across great distances, and many times land on their feet after falling. Cats can hear and scent extremely well and are able to see in almost total darkness. They are among the most agile of animals, as well as one of the best hunters. Plus, they can defend themselves from animals much larger and stronger, due to lightning reflexes and razor-sharp claws and teeth. Finally, they can climb like no other domestic animal. Truly marvelous creatures deserving our respect.

The average cat measures approximately twenty inches in length, with an additional ten inches or so for the tail, weighing in at an average of eight to ten pounds. Many breeds can be larger, and some smaller. All domestic cats have retractable claws on all four feet, which serve as weapons as well as climbing tools. Cats also have a very formidable set of teeth, numbering thirty (compared to the dog's forty-two). These include four razor-sharp canines, able to grab and hold unfortunate prey or to defend the cat against would-be attackers.

The cat's coat can be either long or short, depending on the breed. In addition to keeping your pet warm, preventing dehydration, and minimizing injury from thorny plants, the cat's coat, in conjunction with her loose skin, acts as a protection against would-be predators who, when attempting to bite into the cat's body, usually end up only getting a mouthful of fur and skin. The texture of a cat's coat can vary dramatically from breed to breed. The Persian, for example, has a long, thick, lustrous coat, while the Siamese has a short, fine one. One breed, the Sphynx, has no coat whatsoever, making it susceptible to sunburn.

Cats have marvelously supple, athletic bodies, allowing them to perform amazing feats of agility and strength. The feline skeleton has thirty vertebrae, five more than a human's, allowing much more flexibility and range of movement. Cats shoulder blades are positioned close to the chest, allowing the legs to travel in larger arcs than those of other animals. This, combined with the cat's lack of a collarbone, gives your cat the ability to move more freely than most other mammals.

In comparison to humans, the cat's senses are incredibly developed. The feline eye has proportionately more surface area than the human eye, giving it a wider field of vision. The pupil, in charge of controlling the amount of light entering the eye, gives the cat that slit-eyed look, especially under bright conditions, when it closes down. The real magic of the cat eye, though, is in the construction of the retina, the back, inner surface of the eye that acts like film in a camera, accepting focused images from the lens and transforming them into electronic impulses for the brain to sort out. A cat's retina has a reflective coating behind it called the *tapetum lucidum*, which reflects back onto the retina any light not absorbed the first time around. This allows the cat to use more of the available light. Though unable to see in total darkness, cats can see under lighting conditions that we would consider to be pitch-black. The *tapetum lucidum* also gives the cat's eyes that captivating "glow in the dark" feature, also present in other species, including the dog. The cat eye does not see as clearly as a human eye but does detect movement better. Though cats can distinguish color on a very basic level, they cannot do so nearly as well as humans. The reason for this is simply that felines do not need to do so to survive, whereas humans do, to locate colorful fruits and vegetables and to distinguish poisonous foods and animals from less dangerous ones. Cats are carnivorous, and need eyesight that specializes in catching dull-colored, fast-moving prey.

Cats have excellent hearing, a product of having to listen for the nearly silent movements of rodents scurrying about. Capable of hearing sounds much higher than we can, the feline ear is even more sensitive than that of the dog. In addition, the cat is able to move each ear independent of the other, so as to pinpoint exactly where a sound is coming from. The most amazing fact about the feline ear, however, has to do with its relationship to balance and spatial orientation, which is much more three-dimensional than our own. Like ourselves, cats have semicircular liquid-filled canals in their inner ears. Unlike us, however, these canals are situated at right angles to each other, allowing the cat's brain to better determine change in the body's rotational attitude and direction. Combined with the cat's amazing body, this phenomenon gives cats their famous "righting ability," allowing them to land on all four feet no matter what their initial positioning was.

Though not as sensitive as the dog's, the cat's sense of smell is more acute than our own. The sinus cavities of a cat are quite large, allowing inhaled scent molecules to be analyzed quickly and efficiently. Cats do not rely on their sense of smell nearly as much as vision and hearing, however, when it comes to hunting. The sense of smell seems to be more crucial in locating other cats, though, for mating purposes or for territorial recognition.

A cat's sense of taste is well developed, though no taste buds for sweetness exist on the feline tongue. Carnivores like the cat have little need to detect sweetness, unlike vegetarians and omnivores, who routinely eat plant materials that have moderate to high levels of sugar in them.

A cat's sense of touch is well developed and important. Cats use their paws, covered with touch receptors, to touch and investigate objects nearly as much as humans use their hands. Anyone who has ever owned a cat will know this to be true and will recall being touched on the face by the cat's paw on many occasions. This is different than with dogs, who rarely uses their paws to probe an object or affectionately touch an owner's face. The cat's skin is also covered with many touch receptors, causing even the slightest touch to evoke a reaction. In addition, the cat's whiskers (located on the muzzle, eyebrows, and elbows) provide cats with much information about their world. Attached directly to sensitive nerve bundles, the whiskers transmit information not only about available space but also about subtle changes in air currents, which could denote the presence of a prey animal or an obstacle, when no light is available for the cat to use his or her vision.

Cats are among the fastest mammals. Their reflexes are much quicker than ours. They need to be if cats are to catch fast little rodents. The reason for the cat's quickness is the high number of fast-twitch muscle fibers present in the muscles. Like a sprinter rather than a long-distance runner, the cat can move like lightning but doesn't have great endurance (unlike the dog), which may be one of the reasons that most cats despise swimming. It takes great endurance and relies little on speed.

ARE CATS REALLY "DOMESTICATED"?

Unlike the dog, whose history of domestication goes back far longer than that of the cat, the cat really didn't begin to develop a real working relationship with humans until the emergence of organized agriculture. Once we began harvesting and storing grain, rodents began to become a nuisance, breaking into storage facilities and eating up the precious contents, as well as spreading disease.

Enter the cat. Ancient agricultural cultures began using cats to extinguish the rodent populations, which, if not controlled, could threaten the very existence of the community. Efficient hunters of rodents and other small vermin, cats helped preserve needed food supplies and kept rodent-borne diseases at a minimum. They didn't even have to be trained to do it; they just followed their instincts. And so the so-called domestication of the cat began.

Because rodents control was all cats were needed for, they never became as genetically manipulated as the dog, who had to take on many different duties, from guarding and herding to tracking, hunting, and even racing. Dogs went on to become much more malleable, controlled creatures, while cats were allowed to keep most of their wild instincts intact. The fact that dogs are primarily pack animals, with a strong desire to fit in and obey whoever they think is the leader, also made them much more tractable, reliable servants. The cat's independent nature has allowed them to remain the same aloof, self-motivating animals they have always been, able to slip back and forth from the edges of the wild to your home with little effort at all. In answer to the question: "Are cats really domesticated?" one would have to say, "Yes, as long as it suits them to be so!"

THE CAT/OWNER RELATIONSHIP: WHO ARE WE TO THEM?

Cats, though extremely self-reliant, will nonetheless show their owners much affection, when it suits their fancy. Anyone who has ever owned a cat can tell you that cats may walk up to you and softly touch their paw to your face, or rub up against you while purring quietly, both signs of familiarity and love. Actually, most cats will display much more affection toward humans than they will for their own kind. This most likely has much to do with their not viewing us as competitors for food, shelter, territory, sex, or anything else that cats covet when among themselves. Because of this (as well as the fact that we often neuter our cats at a relatively young age), our cats remain in a quasi-juvenile state of mind for most of their lives, at least with regard to us. We don't ever create for them an atmosphere of competition or of impending adulthood. We allow them to stay kids forever, which in turn allows them to show us the affection that only a parent or sibling could ever expect. It seems as if we are nonthreatening members of their family, toward whom they feel nothing but affection and trust.

THE IMPORTANCE OF UNDERSTANDING A CAT'S NEEDS AND DESIRES

In order to be happy, healthy, and free of undesirable behaviors, your cat has to have certain basic needs met. Most owners are aware of some, while other needs might not be so obvious. As one of the main themes of this book is prevention, it makes sense to briefly talk about what a cat's basic needs and desires might be. Doing your best to provide your cat with all of them can help prevent a host of problems before they ever surface.

Food
This is an obvious need, as your cat must have sufficient food each day in order to stay happy and healthy not only for nutritional reasons but also to satisfy his food/prey drive. Most owners supply their cats with more than enough food. As much care must be taken, however, with regard to the quality of the food as to the quantity. A cat who eats plenty of poor quality food will become just as malnourished as a cat who doesn't eat enough quality food. Without the right nutrition, a cat will suffer and show both physiological and behavioral signs of it.

Shelter

This is another no-brainer, as all cats need to be sheltered from inclement weather, harsh temperatures, or any other severe conditions that might threaten their health and well-being. Most owners of indoor cats need not fret over this one. Cats allowed to go outdoors, however, could on occasion find themselves caught in brutal conditions. As an owner, your job is to see that this does not occur.

A Clean Environment

Cats are among the most fastidious of animals. They keep themselves very clean and prefer their living quarters to be the same. Owners who do not provide this for their cats run the risk of inducing undesirable behaviors in them. For example, an owner who does not regularly scoop his or her cat's litter box out will eventually cause the cat's house-training habits to take a turn for the worse. No longer willing to tolerate the filthy box, the cat will choose another less offensive spot in the home to eliminate in. Even after the owner cleans the offending litter box out and refills it with clean litter, the cat may refuse to use it again, preferring to use the corner of a closet or a pile of clean clothes instead. When your cat decides against something, it is very hard to change his mind. The best way, then, to avoid this type of problem is to keep the cat's environment as clean as possible.

Stability

Cats hate change. Ask any cat owner who has moved into a new home after living in the old one for the entire life of the pet. Suddenly shift a ten-year-old tabby to a completely new territory, miles away from the old one, with strange new smells and scary new sounds outside, and you could be asking for trouble. Cats become very set in their ways and strongly dislike being uprooted. Even bringing in a new piece of furniture or changing the carpeting or drapes can often cause a normally well behaved cat to misbehave. Though it is impractical to expect you to never change your environment, keep in mind that, when making changes, you should expect some unusual behavior to follow. This instruction applies not only to the physical environment of the pet but to the structure of the day as well. For example, if you are never home during the day, then suddenly change to working nights, your cat will react to it in some way, be it a temporary moodiness, a quick bout of house-training mishaps, or something equally undesirable.

Bringing new pets into the home is also a challenge. Your cat needs to feel as little territorial competition as possible if he's going to maintain an acceptable level of behavior. Remember, cats are even more territorial than dogs; a cat's suddenly having to share his domain with another cat or dog can cause aggression, housetraining mishaps, and destruction to your property. Marking territory, scratching furniture, and full-out fighting will often erupt when you ask your mature cat to share his space. If you want two cats, get them both as kittens, instead of having one for years, then getting another. The same goes for owning a dog; get a puppy at the same time you get a kitten. Raised together, they will get along just fine.

Get one, then the other years later, and you're just asking for trouble.

Even bringing in a new person into the home can alter a cat's behavior for a while. It can be difficult for some cats to adjust, especially the shy, timid types.

The bottom line is, change what must be changed, but otherwise keep the status quo, so as to allow your cat to feel the stability he instinctively seeks in his environment.

Training Your Cat: Is it Possible?

Though not as trainable as dogs, cats are great problem solvers and seem to be better at three-dimensional thought than their canine cousins, due most likely to their climbing and leaping abilities. Cats do very well in maze experiments and seem to remember information for a very long time. Clearly they are intelligent and capable of learning a wealth of behaviors.

Animal trainers for television and film have known the key to training cats for years. Simply put, that secret is food, the biggest motivator in a cat's life. A wealth of behaviors can be taught to a cat by simple bribery. Trainers simply put a cat on a regular feeding schedule (instead of free-feeding), then work the behavior right before feeding time, using food rewards as reinforcement for the desired response. The desire to receive those tasty tidbits spurs most cats on to perform.

Also essential to any type of training success is starting the cat out early in life. Adult cats not used to performing for a meal usually don't have the ability to learn behaviors very well, compared to those cats conditioned to perform for food from a young age. Begun early enough and conditioned to work for food, most cats can learn to perform a wide variety of behaviors, including come, sit, down, stay, fetch, and many others normally considered teachable only to dogs. So, in answer to the question, cats can be trained to perform a wealth of behaviors, provided the right techniques are used at the right time.

Thinking like a Cat: Understanding Why Undesirable Behaviors Occur

Whenever some behavior of your cat clashes with your expectations, she is said to be misbehaving. The cat might not think of her behavior as being improper. She might not see anything wrong with it at all. For instance, marking, scratching, and stalking behaviors are all natural, normal behaviors for cats. For your cat to scratch up the back of your sofa or hungrily chase your guinea pig all around the house seems normal to her. She in no way means for them to be malicious acts, intended to annoy you.

When you ask your cat not to perform an instinctive behavior, you are going up against millions of years of evolution. So, one major cause of misbehavior in a cat is caused not by the pet's desire to consciously annoy you but by the owner's inability to find a way for the cat to express those natural instincts in an acceptable way or to cleverly let the animal know what the new rules are concerning good and bad behavior in the home.

The undesirable behavior of ripping up the back of a sofa, for instance, can easily be stopped by providing the cat with several scratching posts, particularly in areas where the cat tends to nap, as cats love to scratch right after waking. This redirection of the natural instinct is a much better solution to the sofa destruction than any overt punishment ever could be. The cat continues the behavior, only in a different, more acceptable place.

One way to help minimize bad behaviors in your cat is to try to think like she would. If you were a cat, wouldn't you find that tiny parakeet a tremendous temptation, especially with it sitting atop the easily accessible dresser, with those flimsy metal bars spaced so wide apart? Doesn't that messy, half-filled, unscooped litter box look much less appealing than the nice potting soil in that huge ficus tree pot over in the corner of the bedroom? Scratch one frightened bird. Pull out the vacuum cleaner for that dirty mess on the carpet. These misbehaviors could have been easily avoided by your looking around the home through the eyes of a cat and seeing the temptations. The parakeet should have been located in a cat-proof area (good luck with that one), and the litter box should have been kept clean and full. End of problems before they start.

In addition to prevention, other ways to avoid cat misbehaviors exist. Again, think like a cat; do you want to have absolutely nothing to do all day? If you do not supply your cat with adequate and acceptable distractions, she will find ways to entertain herself that might not meet with your approval. The bored cat will end up getting into cupboards, closets, and other areas you consider off-limits, simply out of a need to satisfy her instinct to be curious about her environment. Get down on all fours and think like a cat; what is there to investigate?

Instead of letting your cat decide, provide her with interesting distractions that will keep her attentions off areas and objects you want left alone. A cardboard box filled with newspaper. A carpeted, three-tiered play station. A few squeeze toys. Some catnip toys. Whatever your cat finds interesting. By providing her with plenty of behavioral enrichment in this way, you will be distracting her away from those things you want left alone.

If you first make an effort to understand the root causes of your cat's misbehavior, then take steps to prevent it from occurring again, you and your feline friend will have a much happier relationship. Just remember that the cat isn't acting out of malice or spite; she's just doing what she thinks is necessary and what her instincts tell her to do. Thinking like a cat and staying one step ahead of her will cut most bad behaviors off at the pass.

Effective Techniques for Ending an Undesirable Feline Behavior

Because of cats' aversion to change, dealing with a misbehaving cat isn't always that easy. Expect a cat to respond like a dog, and you'll be in for a surprise. In trying to rid yourself of one problem you might end up creating two new ones. Cats just won't deal well with an owner who tries some type of confrontational behavior modification technique. So what's an owner to do?

Partly the solution lies in understanding that though cats do want to get along peaceably with their owners, they also do not want to "lose face" or overtly submit to another's will. This sense of self-determination in your cat runs deep; try to openly challenge or destroy this, and the cat will react badly. A much better way to change your cat's behavior is to do so in such a manner as to convince him that it was *his choice to change*. Let him think it was all his decision. For instance, if your bored cat has begun to climb the curtains in an effort to entertain himself, all you need do is add some entertaining props, such as a carpeted multilevel kitty condo, to the cat's environment to redirect his behavior. The key to this solution is that the cat would think that *he made the choice to leave the curtains alone,* in favor of the new plaything. Because he decided to redirect himself, there is no stress or trauma involved. End of problem; everyone is happy. You *prevented* the offensive behavior by *distracting* your cat's attention from the curtains and onto the kitty condo.

Another effective tactic is to simply identify the cause of an offensive behavior and *remove* it from the pet's environment. For instance, if your cat has taken to chewing away on one of your houseplants, all you need do is remove it from the pet's environment. Then, if you like, you can substitute a small pot of alfalfa or some other type of cat-friendly grass, allowing the cat to satisfy his craving for greens, which cats do get from time to time. Again, there was never any confrontation between you and the cat; as far as he knows, it was all his decision.

Another way to change your cat's behavior nonconfrontationally is *desensitizing* her to a potentially upsetting stimulus. For instance, if she seems to be rather shy around a person other than yourself, you might try having the person come over on a regular basis, at dinnertime, and prepare and serve the cat her food. She will quickly begin to associate the presence of the new person with what might be her favorite time of the day and eventually grow to look forward to the "interloper's" presence. The reserved behavior is modified in a nonconfrontational way.

When passive, nonconfrontational methods fail, mild forms of *discouragement* may need to be utilized to end the offensive behavior. For instance, if, despite the fact that you have supplied your cat with numerous scratching posts throughout the home, she insists on continuing to scratch the back of your expensive sofa, a timely squirt of water from a spray bottle or water pistol can help minimize or end the behavior. If every time she attempts to scratch the furniture she gets a sudden stream of water in the face or backside, she will begin to think twice about continuing the unwanted action. The beauty of the spray bottle technique is that the unpleasant consequence (namely, the stream of water) in no way jeopardizes the trust the cat has in you. Cats who are physically abused by their owners become fearful of them and will never feel at ease again when their masters are close by. This sabotages the cat/owner relationship. The squirt of water, though shocking, is a separate entity from your own body. Even combining it with a firm *No!* command won't cause your cat to fear your presence or touch. He will only become conditioned to the word itself, quickly realizing that *No!* means *"you are doing something wrong and should stop it now."* The cat will quickly end the undesirable behavior to avoid the mysterious stream of water.

To review, minimizing undesirable behaviors in your cat (while still maintaining a good relationship with him) requires some thinking ahead and a real understanding of the feline psyche. To effectively modify a cat's behavior, you should try these techniques, in the following order:

1. *Prevent,* by not introducing disturbing stimuli into the cat's environment.
2. *Distract,* by introducing a better, more acceptable stimulus into the cat's life.
3. *Remove,* if possible, whatever stimulus is causing the inappropriate behavior.
4. *Desensitize* your cat to whatever is causing her to misbehave.
5. *Discourage* her from behaving improperly by using benign, impersonal methods such as a water pistol squirt from across the room.

Why Overt Punishment Won't Work

In order to happily live with your cat, you must develop a bond of mutual trust. He must know that *at no time* will you (an animal ten or fifteen times his size) physically abuse or frighten him. Cats, unlike dogs, will hold a grudge; mistreat your cat once, and he may never forgive you. He may not necessarily stop the offending behavior, either, and could develop a few more as a result of the confrontation. Cats tend to "shut down" when presented with any type of ultimatum or overt threat. Scream at your cat, or swat him off the sofa with your hand, and he will shut down his cognitive processes and begin to fear you. Instead of ending the undesirable behavior, you will destroy the relationship and create great stress in his life. The *only* time an owner should ever consider yelling at or striking a cat is if the pet is in the process of physically harming you or a loved one. Of course, if the pet's behavior has degenerated to that level, one must ask oneself why that is and whether the relationship is even worth maintaining.

The Effects of Health on Behavior

Unlike humans, cats tend to be rather stoic when it comes to showing pain or discomfort. They hide sickness or injury well; often an owner won't have a clue that his or her cat is ill or hurting in any way. Even cats struck by cars will often show no obvious signs of injury, save an increased desire to sleep or a sudden need to hide themselves away somewhere.

Many unusual and undesirable feline behaviors can be caused by some form of physical problem. The stress your cat feels from being sick or injured can often drive her to act in an unusual way. For instance, many cats, upon contracting some type of viral or bacterial infection, may suddenly begin to eliminate outside the litter box. Other than this symptom, however, the cat might not show any other outward signs of illness.

Before trying to correct some undesirable behavior in your cat, consider the fact that she may be suffering from illness or injury. Many unusual behaviors can be halted and corrected simply by having an examination performed by your veterinarian. Doing so could end the undesirable behavior and possibly save your cat's life in the process. So remember: always ensure that your cat is healthy first, before trying to effect some behavioral change.

To do so, you need to have a competent, caring veterinarian available. What qualities should you look for in a veterinarian? Beyond having a true love for animals, he or she should:

◆ Be knowledgeable and have a desire to keep up with the latest trends in pet health care.
◆ Communicate well with owners and never seem rushed, impatient, or rude.
◆ Allow you to be present during your cat's preliminary examination (though do not expect to be able to stick around during surgeries or any type of emergency procedure).
◆ Be organized and professional. The premises should not be dirty or chaotic, and the staff should be polite and helpful.
◆ Be reasonably priced. Though cost is often the furthest thing from your mind when your pet is ill, it nevertheless can become an issue. Veterinarians who charge outrageous fees for standard procedures such as neutering or vaccinating should be

avoided, as should budget, high-volume
clinics that appear too inexpensive to be
true.

Finding a good veterinarian can often be as easy
as getting a referral from a trusted friend or relative.
Talking to your local shelter or listening to your
breeder's advice can also be a good way to locate a
competent veterinarian. You can even look in the local yellow pages, though this can often be a hit-and-
miss affair and will require you to visit several clinics
in advance in order to make an enlightened choice.

Once you have found an acceptable veterinarian,
be sure to take your cat in for an annual checkup to
head off illness at the pass and ensure the continuation
of your cat's good health. Take your pet in once par
year, even if he appears in perfect health. The doctor
will check all of the cat's vital signs, examine him for
any abnormal lumps, growths, or parasites, and listen
to his heart and lungs. He or she might also perform
blood, fecal, or urine tests, to confirm good health or
to catch a problem before it becomes serious. Vacci-
nations will also be given, to ensure that your pet is
immunized against all possible life-threatening contagions. This is especially important for cats who
spend any time outdoors.

Make Training Fun

If your cat does exhibit one or more of the behavior
problems listed in part 2 of this book, it won't be the
end of the world. Each listing will clearly lay out for
the reader the steps he or she will need to take to

eliminate the problem, as well as a way to prevent it from ever recurring. Throughout the process of ridding your cat of one or more of these behavioral problems, try not to become too serious or confrontational; remember that she is just a cat, with the reasoning capacity of a two-year-old child at best. She doesn't initially know that the behavior is improper. Look upon the situation as an opportunity to learn about your cat and yourself. See it as a valuable learning experience that opens up a window on feline instincts and behavior that might have previously been closed to you. Try to enjoy the experience; no one says you can't have fun reeducating your cat, which may be the key to success. Keep things in perspective, and make sure that both you and your pet have a good time learning about each other. In doing so you will increase your chances of success a hundredfold and develop an even closer bond with your little friend.

PART TWO

Cat Behavior Problems, A–Z

The heart of the book, this section lists the most common behavior problems evident in today's domestic cats and offers solutions that any owner should be able to implement. Each alphabetical listing will include:

1. The *name* of the undesirable behavior.
2. A detailed *description* of the behavior, enabling the cat owner to quickly determine if this is what his or her cat is doing wrong.
3. An explanation of *why the behavior is occurring,* to aid you in understanding the behavior from the cat's perspective.
4. An easily implemented *solution* designed to minimize the offending behavior and prevent it from recurring and *preventive* suggestions that will block the behavior from surfacing in the first place.

AGGRESSION

DESCRIPTION

Aggression can be defined as an offensive or defensive attack on an animal or human, with the intention of dominating, scaring off, intimidating, hurting, or even killing the unfortunate "invader." Several different types of aggression might be seen in a domestic cat, including:

1. *Dominance (or territorial) aggression,* in which the offending cat uses force or intimidation to control others and to possess whatever he or she desires.
2. *Fear aggression,* in which the cat attacks when frightened.
3. *Food aggression,* in which the cat attacks in order to protect his or her food or to take that of another.
4. *Hereditary aggression,* caused by faulty breeding.
5. *Maternal and paternal aggression,* in which a feline mother defends her kittens or an unneutered male (or tom) cat kills kittens sired by another tom.
6. *Prey aggression,* as evidenced by a cat stalking and/or killing another animal.
7. *Sexual aggression,* which takes place between a female and a male cat during courtship.
8. *Play aggression,* usually evidenced by a kitten or adolescent cat.
9. *Redirected aggression,* in which a stressed cat lashes out at an innocent.

Whatever form of aggression your cat might be evidencing, it is never a pleasant experience, for the owner or the cat. Often predictable and unavoidable, aggression needn't be a symptom of a disturbed pet but can actually be an understandable and proper response to certain situations. For instance, if your cat is nursing kittens and a happy-but-foolish golden retriever puppy comes bounding into the room to investigate, that silly young canine is going to feel that mother cat's wrath mighty quickly, and rightly so. She is totally within her rights to protect her kittens from what she deems a possible threat to them from an adversary. In this case, the maternal aggression shown by her would be totally justifiable and natural. Any attempts to curb this form of aggression on your part would be unfair to the cat and would cause undue stress and anxiety for all. A cat forced into a totally alien environment (perhaps a friend's home) and surrounded by strangers might justifiably show some fear aggression toward these unknown characters, out of an instinct for self-preservation.

Though some aggression seen in domestic cats is explainable and normal, other forms of aggression can be quite abnormal. Abnormally timid cats, for instance, might fear anything out of the ordinary and react aggressively when they needn't. Many timid cats, for instance, have been known to scratch and injure human babies or toddlers, who, though meaning no overt harm, can seem very unpredictable and threatening to an inherently fearful cat. Overly dominant cats might actually go out of their way to attack another animal (or even a human) if they feel that their territory is being threatened in any way. Allowable in the wild, perhaps, this behavior is not welcome within the confines of domesticity. Domestication, in fact, is the key factor that can bring cat aggression to the forefront; in our desire to tame and subjugate our cats to life in a home filled with adults, children, visitors, dogs and other cats, noise, and all manner of "unnatural" stimuli (from the cat's point of view), we have unintentionally created a potentially stressful environment for our felines, who are programmed to exist in a less frenetic and social world.

Whether normal or abnormal, feline aggression can be very upsetting to an owner who does not understand it or is not prepared for it. How an owner reacts to his or her cat's aggression is also an important issue; overreaction or improper responses can actually intensify the aggressive problem.

Being able to identify and deal with the different forms of feline aggression will make you a better owner. To that end, explanations and solutions for each of the nine basic types of aggression will be given, so that you might recognize which one your cat is exhibiting.

WHY YOUR CAT IS DOING THIS

Dominance-territorial aggression occurs when your cat feels that his status or territory is being usurped by another animal, often a fellow cat. The aggressive cat will hiss at, chase, or physically attack the intruder. Often his ears will point up, his tail will lash back and forth erratically, and his hair will stand on end, in an effort to make him appear larger and more formidable.

Cats are still not nearly as sociable as dogs, who yearn for the companionship of others. By and large, cats are at best uncomfortably tolerant of others attempting to share their domains, with the exception of their owners, whom they see as siblings or parents.

Your little house cat has all the same territorial instincts as any wild feline. Your home is his territory; any time an unknown creature comes around, it will initially be seen by your cat as an intruder. Though most domesticated cats won't necessarily apply this rationale to human visitors, they will nonetheless probably decide to be a bit aloof toward your friends and relatives, at least for a short while.

Your cat will certainly see a dog or another cat as an intruder, however, especially if he is an adult. Some level of aggression, at least in the beginning, should be expected. Though it may not escalate past hissing and swatting, it could, and you need to be prepared for that.

Apart from territorial concerns, your cat may want to express his status, or dominance, over the intruding animal (or person). Though not normally pack-oriented, cats are still motivated by a hierarchical concerns when placed into any social situation. Whenever two or more adult cats get together, for instance, they will immediately begin working out who is the more dominant of the two, much as dogs will do. Cats tend not to be quite as civil or tolerant as dogs, however, simply because they aren't as practiced at it. Kittens are better at tolerating others of their own kind, because they either are still in the litter or have just recently left their siblings, whose memories and influences are still fresh in their minds. Once they are four to five months old, however, the more solitary mindset kicks in, making dominance contests with other cats more likely.

In general, cat aggression motivated by dominance or territorial issues isn't usually a life-threatening issue and often works itself out without much input from the owner. Cat-to-cat aggression of this type is often limited to some posturing, hissing, and perhaps a few well-timed swats from the more dominant animal. Cat-to-dog aggression can be more serious, for obvious reasons; most dogs are larger than most cats and may respond to a cat's dominance or territorial aggression by turning on their prey drive or by invoking their own territorial, dominant mind-set. If either of these occur, it could be curtains for the cat. If the dog in question is a friendly one, he or she may trustingly get too close to a wary cat and get scratched. Though this usually doesn't have dire consequences, the dog's eyes can be in danger.

Rarely will a cat be overtly territorial or dominant over a human; when it does happen, it's normally a sign of an extremely pushy cat. More often, cat aggression toward a human will be of a type other than dominance or territorial.

Fear aggression occurs in your cat when he decides that something is not only threatening to his safety but also unavoidable, causing him to fight rather than flee. A cat displaying fear aggression will exhibit clear body language cues, including:

- Ears flat against the head
- Hair standing on end
- Pupils dilated
- Tail thrashing back and forth
- Hissing
- Usage of the front paws, usually to lash out at the threat
- Arched back
- Slow retreating movement, often followed by a quick attack

In addition, some fearful cats, when left no other recourse, will go belly-up and brandish all four paws up into the air, razor-sharp claws ready to slash away at the attacker. Often children and dogs will mistake this posture as an inviting, playful one, only to find out otherwise upon approaching the cat.

Fear-aggressive cats will strike out at anyone or anything that comes inside what they decide is their "safe space." Should a person, child, dog, or other pet try to approach too closely, fear-aggressive felines may hiss, scratch or even bite the perceived intruder, even though no real threat was intended. It's what the cat decides is dangerous and not the well-meaning approacher.

The level of socialization that kittens receive while still in the litter plays a huge role in determining whether they will show signs of excess fear aggression later in life. Kittens who are separated from the litter before the eighth week, for instance, often become antisocial, fearful, and timid adults. The fifth through the eighth weeks are especially crucial; during this time, they learn how to properly interact with other cats. If robbed of this key experience, a cat will almost always suffer from some form of behavioral problem later on.

Bad experiences can also trigger fear aggression in a cat. Felines have amazing powers of recall; if a young child accidentally tripped over your four-month-old kitten, injuring her in the process, the cat will remember the experience forever and very likely be uneasy around children for her entire life. Likewise your otherwise well adjusted cat attacked by a dog will almost always show profound fear around other dogs for the rest of his days.

Food aggression is much less common in cats than in dogs, whose wild cousins tend to gorge-eat more than do cats in the wild. Wild felines will more often make numerous kills of smaller prey animals during the day than canines, who tend to kill larger animals on a less frequent basis, making it necessary to eat very large amounts of meat, when available. Dogs therefore have more of a drive to eat when food is available.

A cat will show food aggression, however, under several circumstances. If your cat has spent part of his life as a stray, odds are he had to learn to fight for his meals. Food was scarce; any little morsel might have made the difference between life and death. Bring this stray cat into your home, then, and you might find that he trounces on your other cat at dinnertime, completely bullying the cat, and hogging the food dish. Shelter cats may very well have the same mind-set; many of them came from the streets or from unappreciative homes, where food might not have been provided regularly.

Food aggression can also occur because of dominance issues. If one cat is clearly dominant over another, chances are that the two won't exhibit much food aggression at all, once an initial confrontation has occurred. The dominant cat quickly lets the submissive one know who's boss and then always feeds first, with no further arguments. The dominant one may even allow the submissive cat access to the dish at the same time. The problem comes when you own two cats who are very close in stature and have not yet been able to resolve the dominance issue. Food becomes a great bone of contention between them. Dinnertime becomes a struggle to dominate, rather than an enjoyable experience. One cat will swat at the other, who then returns the favor. Often it can escalate to a full-out battle, with possible injury to both cats.

Less frequently, a real bully of a cat might exert his dominance over a less domineering cat at dinnertime and not know when to stop the intimidation. The attacked cat becomes frightened and goes into fear mode, causing him to go into a defensive posture. One cat is fighting due to an inflated sense of importance, while the other is fighting out of terror. A nasty scene can ensue.

Hereditary aggression occurs in an unpredictable manner. If your cat has exhibited unpredictable aggressive tendencies from the time you acquired her, she might simply be genetically predisposed to act in this manner. No outside stimuli can be blamed for the problem, though certain situations can trigger aggressive outbursts. A stranger walking too close to the cat, a child innocently trying to pet her, or even an unexpected noise can all set off a cat with this problem. Again, the root cause of hereditary aggression is biological, not environmental.

Maternal aggression can occur whenever someone or something comes too close to a mother cat's litter, particularly when the kittens are newborns. The aggression might even be directed at you, the owner, if the cat feels you are taking too many liberties with her kittens. She may swat at you, hiss, scratch, or even bite repeatedly until you (or whoever she deems a threat) retreat to a "safe" distance. This ancient instinct serves to help preserve the species and ensure that the genes of the parents are passed on. Whether a mother cat is wild or domestic, the same protective instinct will usually be exhibited if she perceives any threat to her kittens.

Maternal aggression in domestic cats is unpredictable. Some feline mothers will become extremely agitated and defensive upon your approach, while others don't seem to care at all. A few cats, particularly those under a year in age, show poor mothering skills and can even abandon a litter, leaving the owner to raise them. Stray cats, often preoccupied with their own survival, will sometimes abandon a litter in order to ensure their own survival.

Most feline mothers have a good sense of who is

and who isn't a threat to their kittens, however. As many owners are seen as parents by their cats, a nesting mother will often allow an owner contact with the litter, out of parental respect. Let a dog or another cat get too close, however, and that same sweet female will probably turn into a buzz saw.

Paternal aggression occurs both in the wild and in domesticity. Male cats sometimes kill the kittens of a nesting female who mated with one of their competitors. They wait for an opportunity to arise, then sneak in and kill the entire litter. Male cats exhibit paternal aggression for a simple reason: by killing a competitor's kittens, the male cat prevents that competitor's genes from being passed on. Also, after the kittens are dead the female will rapidly come back into heat, opening up the opportunity for the murderous male to mate with her and spread his genes.

Prey aggression occurs most often with cats allowed outdoors. If your cat regularly attempts to stalk small animals or even seems to be taking great interest in your parakeet or hamster, odds are she is exhibiting a normal level of prey drive. If you allow your cat outdoors, don't be shocked when she begins to show up with mice and baby birds in her mouth. The reason for this is simple: cats are born predators. Whether neutered or not, both males and females will exhibit some level of predatory drive on a regular basis. Aggression toward a prey animal is a normal instinct that cannot be modified and should not be deemed distasteful, even though finding dead rodents and birds outside the door (or in the home) can be upsetting, to say the least. Unneutered cats will exhibit prey ag-

gression more keenly, as will cats allowed to go outdoors from an early age.

Sexual aggression can be a hard one for owners to
tolerate. During mating, after initially rejecting the
male's sexual approaches, the female eventually allows him to grasp her by the nape of the neck and
mount her. The actual act does not contain any overt
aggression, apart from the male's restraint of the female. It is only toward the end that the real conflict
can occur. The male's penis has spines on it that are
thought to help stimulation ovulation in the female.
When the penis is removed, these spines evidently
cause the female a great deal of pain. She will usually
scream, then turn on the male, slashing out at him in
anger. Within a few minutes, however, the entire mating process will often begin anew, with either the
same male or a different partner. Each time, the procedure ends with the female lashing out in pain at the
male. The biting of the female's neck by the male, as
well as the pain-induced lashing out of the female, are
both normal behaviors associated with cat courtship.
You should not try to modify the behavior, as it is
millions of years old and part of the process. What
you should be asking yourself is this: why am I allowing my cat to breed? If you are not a licensed and
experienced cat breeder, you shouldn't be letting your
pet breed at all. Too many unwanted kittens and cats
are put to death each year to warrant the haphazard
breeding of any more.

Play aggression occurs mostly in young cats. During the first few months of life, kittens learn to stalk
and attack primarily through playing with their litter-

mates. They will take turns sneaking up on each other from all angles, pouncing on an unsuspecting brother or sister whenever possible. If your cat has maintained a juvenile, kittenish mind-set into adulthood, he may still be exhibiting this playful stalking and pouncing behavior, directed toward either other pets in the home or even you, a family member, or a visitor. No actual harm comes to the "victim"; it is just a game that the attacker has loved to play since kittenhood. After the mock attack, the aggressor cat usually is as friendly as can be. Cats who maintain this juvenile mind-set will act like kittens much of the time. They will knead at you with their front paws the way kittens do to their mothers when nursing (thought to help stimulate milk production in the mother) and remain much more sociable than an adult cat would ordinarily be. They will also continue to play kittenish games, including the stalking and pouncing game.

Redirected aggression can occur in stressed cats. Have you ever tried to mediate an argument between two friends, only to have them both attack you? Or have you ever gotten so angry over something that you ended up taking out your frustrations on another person, even though he or she might have had nothing to do with it? These are perfect examples of redirected aggression. You can't do anything about the problem itself, so you simply vent your anger on the nearest vulnerable victim.

Cats are very capable of this type of aggression. For instance, have you ever tried to break up a cat fight? If so, you may have had one or both of the cats actually attack you instead of each other. That's redirected aggression. Both know that you are an easy, harmless target for their tensions and fears; attacking you is a release for them. Another example is when your cat, after being injured, scratches or bites you as you are simply be trying to examine the cat or take him to the veterinarian. The animal is scared and in pain; to release the stress, he attacks you. It is a non-thinking form of aggression very akin to fear aggression. The victim of redirected aggression is usually seen by the cat as a scapegoat or an easy mark.

SOLUTION

Successfully reducing or eliminating aggression in your cat depends entirely on what type of aggression is being displayed. The following are possible solutions for each of the aforementioned categories of aggression:

For *dominance/territorial aggression* in your cat, you should:

1. Have your cat neutered before six months of age. Whether your pet is a male or female, allowing him or her to remain unneutered will only encourage dominance/territorial disputes, as well as create tension between you and the pet over issues of excessive marking, scratching, and roaming. Neutering (castrating a male or spaying a female) will remove sexual tensions from

the mix and make it possible for two or
more cats to live side by side in relative
harmony.

2. Keep your cat indoors as much as possible.
Allowing him unlimited access to the
outdoors will ensure that he will eventually
get into numerous fights with other outdoor
pets, causing yours to gradually view any
other cats as dangerous and threatening.
Once that occurs, you may never be able to
successfully socialize him with another
animal.

3. Do your best to keep your cat's home
environment as calm and predictable as
possible to avoid the chance of her
experiencing any traumatic episodes, such
as a group of small children suddenly
chasing her around the house or the
neighbor's Labrador retriever rushing in to
say hi. Remember that cats remember
troubling experiences for a very long time
and often hold grudges against the
offending individuals. Keep things as stable
and predictable as possible, to ensure that
your cat is not presented with a situation in
which she must defend her territory or exert
her dominance over strange invaders.

4. Socialize your cat from as early on as
possible. Allow her to be around different
adults and responsible children right from
the beginning, as well as any other pets you
may have in the home (provided they are

not aggressive themselves). If you want your cat to get along well with another cat or a dog, consider raising them together. Two kittens raised in the same home from the time they are eight to ten weeks old often will get along far better than an established adult and a new kitten or adult cat. Likewise for a dog/cat combo; raise the puppy and kitten together, and odds are they will be the best of friends. Bring a puppy or adult dog into an adult cat's world, however, and you could be in for some real fireworks. Bringing a kitten into the domain of an adult cat could also be potentially disastrous for the kitten, though in all likelihood the young one would simply be put in his or her place right away and then simply treated with a cool indifference.

5. If you do decide to bring a new cat into your resident cat's territory, do so very gradually, by using the following technique:

A. Start by keeping the new pet inside a room with the door closed, for at least a few days. Your resident cat will know that a new animal is present from the scent but will not be able to confront the stranger directly. The new cat will experience the same thing. In this way, you begin to gradually acclimate them to each other.

B. After two or three days of this, place the new cat into a plastic carrier crate (available in all pet shops), then allow the resident cat to come over and meet the new addition, *making sure not to open the crate*. Allow them to investigate each other for five minutes or so. They may show some territorial aggression or might actually show some fear. Chances are, though, with the opportunity to physically interact removed from the equation, they will simply sniff each other out at this stage.

C. After five minutes, separate them, allowing your new cat to be loose inside his own room again. Repeat the crating technique at least six times a day for a few days before moving on.

D. Finally begin to let the cats interact for short periods of time without the use of the crate. Make sure you oversee the meeting, but use caution; you do not want to be scratched or bitten. Do not confine the meeting to one room; instead, give both cats the opportunity to retreat to a different area of the home, if need be, to avoid a fight. During these brief interactions, have a glass of water handy to douse the cats if any fighting should erupt. *Don't break up a cat fight yourself!* Do not expect them to be buddies yet; the most you should hope for is acceptance without violence at this point. After about two minutes of this face-to-face, posturing meeting, retire the new cat to his room again. Repeat the meeting several times a day for a day or two, unless the first meeting proved disastrous. If this was the case, go back to the crate stage for a few days, then try again.

E. Eventually you should be able to release the new cat into the rest of the home on a full-time basis. Make sure that both cats have their own litter boxes, as well as separate food and water dishes, to prevent any food aggression from occurring. It will take weeks for them to come to some form of acceptance, but that will eventually happen. One of the cats will express dominance over the other; once this happens, a détente will be reached, and you should have a reasonably peaceful home.

F. Make sure to pay equal attention to both cats. Do not make the mistake of giving the new boarder more attention, as this could provoke a jealous reaction from the older cat.

6. Choose a kitten who seems to interact with his or her littermates in a reasonable fashion. Avoid overly dominant, pushy kittens who seem to bully the others, as

well as the kittens who shrink away from any confrontation. Pick one who shows curiosity yet knows when to back off. Also, make sure not to take a kitten who was separated from his or her mother and littermates before the eighth week, to ensure the kitten gets the proper maternal care, as well as the right amount of early socialization with his or her siblings.

7. If adopting an adult cat, be sure to observe his or her behavior closely first. Is the cat in with other cats or by himself or herself? Are there any fresh (or old) scars on his or her body? Offer the cat a toy or treat, then take it away, watching for the reaction. If this cat shows any possessiveness, move on to a different cat.

For *fear aggression*, you should:

◆ Make sure not to encourage friends or other visitors to handle or interact with your fearful cat. Simply having someone over is probably contact enough. Let the visitor be in the home, and perhaps have him or her toss a few treats down on the floor whenever present. Even if the cat does not come out to eat them, he will slowly begin to associate visitors with a good thing, namely, treats. By doing this regularly you may be able to ease the cat's fears enough for him to eventually investigate the visitor and perhaps allow a pat on the head. At no time, however, should the visitor try to initiate the contact. Let the cat do that.

◆ Locate a fearful cat's litter box and food and water dishes in low-traffic areas. Do not place the litter box in a guest bathroom, where the cat stands a chance of being trapped inside with a stranger.

◆ Tell children and adults never to chase after your cat or attempt to surprise her in any way.

◆ Consult with your veterinarian, who may be able to prescribe a low dosage of a medication that will help the cat relax.

◆ Choose a kitten carefully. Never buy a pet from a pet store or "backyard breeder," as these venues rarely produce quality cats. Also, do not take a kitten from any breeder who is willing to let the kitten go before the eighth week of life. Kitten need to stay with their mothers and siblings at least that long to receive the proper socialization skills. Also, look for a breeder who allows his or her kittens to socialize regularly with humans from two weeks of age on.

◆ If adopting a kitten or cat from a shelter, choose one who appears confident, friendly, and curious around people and other cats. If the animal shows any timidity or fear, keep looking.

◆ Don't bring a kitten or cat into a frenetic home filled with dogs, cats, humans, and lots of unpredictable goings-on. Try to set up a quiet, predictable environment for your new cat, so that she can acclimate to her new surroundings with as little worry as possible.

◆ Socialize the new kitten as much as possible, as soon as possible. A well-adjusted kitten will show little fear of people and other animals, so take advantage of that and introduce him or her to as many friendly, easygoing individuals as possible. The more socialization the kitten gets early on, the less likely she will be to show any signs of fear aggression later on.

For *food aggression,* try:

◆ Moving your cats to opposite sides of the kitchen. Purchase an extra food and water dish and set each cat up in his own corner. This solution will work with cats who simply do not feel comfortable having another cat so close by during feeding time.

◆ Feeding each cat in a separate room, if the aggression is severe. By doing so you will relieve the stress that your attacked cat has been experiencing, letting him eat in peace. You will also be halting the aggressive behavior of the dominant animal, an important factor, as allowing the behavior to continue only serves to reinforce it all the more.

◆ Feeding your cat his food on an elevated level, if food aggression is occurring between a dog and cat. As your cat is easily able to jump up to a counter several feet above the floor, consider simply feeding him atop a kitchen counter while the dog eats undisturbed below.

For *hereditary aggression,* try:

◆ Taking the offending cat in to your veterinarian, who will help you determine if, in fact, the cat does have a genetic predisposition toward aggression. Sometimes hereditary aggression can be mistaken for fear aggression; your veterinarian will help you make that determination. The root of the problem may also be a medical one; if this is the case, there may be a chance to minimize the problem. For instance, an injured or sick cat might be exhibiting unpredictable aggressive tendencies because of great pain; because of the species's stoic nature, you might not ever be aware of the problem. Ending the pain could cure the aggression.

◆ Asking your veterinarian about the use of tranquilizers and mood-altering drugs to minimize the dangerous behavior. Just as Lithium, Prozac, Xanax, and Valium are used to modulate aberrant human behaviors, so can similar medications be used on cats. The right medication just might reduce the cat's aggressive episodes enough to allow nearly normal relationships to commence, perhaps for the first time.

◆ Avoiding purchasing a cat from an amateur or dishonest breeder. Never purchase a kitten from a "backyard breeder," pet shop, or fly-by-night outfit, as they are all normally driven by profit only and have little or no concern for the genetic stability of the cats they sell. Instead, go to a professional breeder with a good reputation and good referrals. If adopting a cat, do so from a reputable local shelter. Good shelters will be able to screen out defective cats before they are ever seen by the public; odds are any kitten or cat you see there will be mentally sound.

For *maternal aggression*, try:

◆ Waiting for a few weeks and tolerating your cat's uneasiness. Fortunately, maternal aggression tends to subside on its own, after a two- or three-week period. Brought on by hormonal changes initiated by birthing and nursing, these changes begin to subside as the kittens get closer and closer to being weaned.

◆ Spaying your cat, which is definitely the

best way to avoid maternal aggression in your cat. The world has far too many unwanted kittens anyway.

◆ Keeping her indoors, away from roaming tomcats, who can smell a female in heat a mile away.

◆ Providing her with a quiet, warm, secure nesting area if she is about to give birth and then simply allowing her to be a mother to her babies. Intervene only if the kittens are in certain peril or appear sick or injured.

For *paternal aggression,* you should:

◆ Consider having your cat neutered before he becomes sexually mature (usually by the sixth month). By removing hormonal factors from the picture you will effectively prevent your male cat from ever participating in this horrible form of aggression.

◆ Keep him indoors and away from any nesting females to prevent him from getting at any kittens. If you know of any nursing females in the area, make sure that the owner ensures the safety of the kittens by not allowing the nest to be outdoors.

For *prey aggression,* you should:

◆ Have your cat neutered. Doing so will reduce her level of prey drive somewhat and help keep her mind off of her predatory urges.

◆ Consider not allowing your cat to roam freely outdoors. If you do allow her free access to the neighborhood, she may begin to hunt and kill birds, mice, squirrels, rats, moles, snakes, and even baby raccoons or skunks. Each year, millions of these small creatures are needlessly killed by pet cats, who often do not even eat their prizes. If you want to help keep the normal balance of your local ecosystem, consider keeping your cat inside.

◆ Attach a bell to your cat's collar so that prey animals can hear her coming and get to safer ground. Make sure the collar you use is one that stretches easily, so it will slip off of the cat if caught on a tree branch or fence. Avoid a nonstretchable collar, as they have been known to strangle cats caught on a limb or fence top.

◆ Consider not having pets that might be considered delectable to your cat. Rodents, birds, rabbits, ferrets, small reptiles, and fish are all prime candidates. If you must have them, be sure to locate them in an area of the home that the cat has no access to. In addition, place the cage or aquarium in the most inaccessible place you can find (which will he a real challenge, considering the cat's athletic abilities). Place a secure lid on all fish tanks, and consider laying down several strips of doubled-sided transparent tape around all small pet containers. Cats hate the feel of the tape on their feet and will usually want to get off it quickly. You can also purchase commercially available cat repellent spray at your local pet shop and use it around the prey animal's container. As a last resort, consider going to your pet shop and purchasing a product called a Scat Mat. This flat plastic mat has thin wires running through it that, when attached to a power source, carry a slight electrical charge. When your predatory cat approaches a cage or aquarium and steps on the mat, she gets an irritating very low-voltage, (but harmless) shock, causing her to retreat and dissuading her from approaching the area again (at least from that direction). You can also try placing strips of aluminum foil around the cage or aquarium; cats hate walking on it.

For *sexual aggression,* try:

◆ Neutering, which will eliminate any chance of sexual aggression taking place.
◆ Keeping the unneutered pet indoors, especially if she is a female in heat. Keeping an intact male indoors can be messy, however, as he will spray all over the home.

For *play aggression,* try:

◆ Allowing two cats playing roughly to work it out between themselves without your intervention unless one or both cats seem to be in danger.

◆ Clapping your hands together briskly and saying *"No!"* in a fairly stern tone, if the cat play-attacks you too roughly. Never hit the cat or scream at the top of you lungs.

◆ Placing soda cans with twenty small pebbles inside around the home so that one is always close at hand. As soon as you see the cat beginning to stage a mock attack on you, pick up a can and throw it onto the floor near the pet. The raucous sound of the pebbles inside the can will sober the cat right up and stop the unwanted behavior.

◆ Sitting quietly in a chair in your living room with a water pistol or plant sprayer bottle filled with water by your side. If your cat begins to stalk you or another pet in the home, spray her with the pistol or sprayer bottle (which should be set to emit a solid stream of water). Getting a faceful of water once or twice should be enough to eliminate the behavior. Keep a few sprayers around the home for a while, just in case she decides to start up again.

For *redirected aggression,* try:

- ◆ Minimizing the number of cats you have in the home.
- ◆ Throwing a glass of cold water onto two fighting cats, instead of trying to break up the fight yourself.
- ◆ Avoiding picking up your cat if she has just undergone a traumatic experience and is still scared. Instead, let her come to you or else give her a few minutes to calm down before trying to comfort her.
- ◆ Socializing her from an early age, so she won't become stressed out whenever new persons show up at the home.
- ◆ Handling her as much as possible from kittenhood on, to minimize stress from being touched.
- ◆ Making sure your cat's environment is safe and secure to prevent stress and injury.
- ◆ Keeping your cat indoors.
- ◆ Keeping hold of your own temper. Remember that your cat's redirected aggression is a nonthinking, instinctive reaction to pain or fear and not a calculated plot to hurt someone.

ANTISOCIAL BEHAVIOR

DESCRIPTION

Any cat who seems to shy away from the company of humans is thought of as being antisocial. Though cats are normally less social with other cats than dogs are with their fellow canines, the feline who runs away and hides from other cats without any interaction at all is showing antisocial tendencies as well. Antisocial behavior taken to the extreme will inevitably become aggression; here we are differentiating between the two by establishing the reaction to the circumstances. A fearful cat who chooses to run away and hide is being antisocial. A timid, frightened cat who turns to fight is being aggressive.

Any cat who shies away from being touched is showing some antisocial tendencies. Those cats who disappear whenever guests come over are exhibiting a higher level of antisocial behavior, while those cats who refuse to allow their own owners to touch them or even occupy the same room are suffering from an even higher level of antisocial behavior.

WHY YOUR CAT IS DOING THIS

Everyone wants their cats to be as sociable as possible. Unfortunately, that can't always work out, because of either the inherent personality traits of the cat, the behavioral limitations of the breed, or the cat's personal history. A cat might simply have a shy temperament or belong to a breed (such as the Persian) that doesn't enjoy lots of company. Or your cat might prefer to spend time alone due to a bad experience in her past, such as repeated physical abuse from a previous owner or another pet. Whatever the reason, some cats just won't want to be as sociable as you'd like them to be. Remember that felines are by nature more solitary than dogs and that wanting lots of social interaction would be considered abnormal behavior for most cats, except for breeds such as the Siamese, who love attention and can't seem to get enough socialization.

You should expect your cat to show a desire to be with you, however. If she doesn't, something is indeed amiss and should be addressed. She should also at least tolerate guests in the home, particularly those who visit on a regular basis. Don't ask her to quickly warm up to a total stranger, though, particularly one of large stature or someone with a boisterous nature. Young children also can often be hard for some cats to feel comfortable with, unless they act calmly and quietly, without lots of unpredictable motion.

SOLUTION

If your cat shows timidity around most persons, the first thing to do is not force the issue. Don't allow anyone to chase your the cat and pick her up. Instead, let the cat decide if and when she will come over and greet the visitor. You can help her along, though, by allowing the visitor to place a tasty treat onto the floor near where he or she is sitting, in hopes that the cat will eventually come out and eat it. If guests do this each time a they come over, the cat will eventually come to see the presence of a stranger as a good thing.

If children come over, instruct them not to chase after the cat, yell and scream, or run around the home.

Have them act just as an adult would, quietly and calmly. Use the same treat conditioning exercise each time, to teach the cat that kids aren't all that bad. When the cat finally does warm up to the child, make sure that he or she is as gentle as possible. Don't expect your reserved cat to be comfortable with toddlers, though, as they tend to be very grabby and might end up pinching the cat's skin or pulling on her tail or ears.

Antisocial behavior toward other cats will usually work itself out over time. The timid cat will eventually have no choice but to accept the presence of the more outgoing animal. Try not to interfere unless the behavior erupts into violence. To avoid this, make sure to always introduce a new cat into the household slowly, according to the guidelines given in the previous section for territorial aggression.

If you have just adopted a new cat who seems to be avoiding you, give her some time. Even the most timid felines will eventually come around and learn to trust the owner, provided he or she is calm, patient, and gentle. Speak softly to your new cat, offer her treats, and never initiate contact. Wait for her to come to you. She will eventually jump up into your lap when you least expect it, inviting you to pet her. She will also decide when petting time is over. That's OK; let her make that determination. By not forcing the issue you will allow the cat to develop trust in you, the cornerstone to eliminating antisocial behavior. Remove doubt and fear, and the cat will yearn for your touch.

BAD BREATH

DESCRIPTION

Though this sounds humorous, bad breath can and does occur in cats. Any foul or sour smell coming from your cat's mouth can indicate a potentially serious health problem in the making.

WHY YOUR CAT IS DOING THIS

Though obviously not a behavioral problem, feline bad breath can be a problem, and one that might be indicative of a physiological disorder in the making. The first suspect should always be a health problem in the cat's mouth. Bacterial buildup, tartar, plaque, or food lodged between teeth can cause your cat to develop bad breath. Gum disease, abscesses, and oral tumors might also be responsible for a bad odor.

Bad oral odor in your cat could also be caused by a disorder in the pet's gastrointestinal tract. Infection, ulcers, tumors, or severe allergic reaction to a certain type of food could also be the culprit. The food she eats might simply be too odoriferous for your taste. Your cat might even be getting into the garbage without your knowing it.

SOLUTION

The first step to take is to bring your cat to the veterinarian, who will perform a thorough exam to locate the cause. Odds are he or she may want to clean your cat's teeth as part of the solution. If so, allow the procedure, as it will most likely cure the problem while extending the life of your cat's teeth at the same time. Your veterinarian will also be able to spot a more serious physiological problem and may even recommend a different, less odor-producing food.

Keeping your cat's teeth clean will go a long way in preventing bad breath and tooth decay. Brushing a cat's teeth isn't normally an easy task, however; most felines would balk at the suggestion. If you start a kitten out from the beginning, however, you may be able to brush her teeth once a week or so without much objection, provided you do so quickly and painlessly. Your veterinarian can provide you with the proper toothpaste and brush. Start out by gently massaging the young kitten's gums and slowly progress to lightly brushing the teeth with a soft-bristle brush and some vet-approved toothpaste. Don't use human toothpaste, as it can irritate the feline mouth. If you have any problem at all, however, don't proceed, as you might cause your cat to distrust you. Better to let the veterinarian clean your cat's teeth and take the brunt of her displeasure.

Your veterinarian or pet store should also be able to provide you with safe chew toys, which can help keep your cat's teeth clean. Floss-type chews usually work the best, but you may have to try several different designs before finding one that your cat prefers.

BATHING, AVERSION TO

DESCRIPTION

Cats hate being bathed. Most will struggle to extricate themselves from the situation by any means possible. Some will scream and wail, while others may actually scratch and bite their dreaded "tormentor." All in all, not a very pretty scene.

WHY YOUR CAT IS DOING THIS

Like most other cats, your cat has two instincts that are quite strong; one is a penchant for cleaning himself; and the other, a strong dislike for immersion in water. Very few cat species enjoy being in water at all, with a few exceptions, such as the tiger.

SOLUTION

As your cat normally tends to his own hygiene quite well, there probably will only be a few times when you need to bathe him. Flea or tick infestation or contact with a messy, oily or toxic substance might require you to do so. Unfortunately, if your adult cat is like most, he won't much care for being wetted down and lathered up by you or anyone else. Trying to do so, no matter how clever you are, might cause your adult cat to develop a grudge. For this reason, it is often better to simply let a trained groomer bathe your cat. He or she will do a great job and act as a scapegoat for your cat's wrath and indignation.

If you have a young kitten, however, it is possible to teach him to tolerate the process. Place the kitten in a sink or large plastic tub. Make sure whatever vessel you use has a rubber mat securely fastened to the inside bottom, to give the concerned kitty something to hold onto with his claws. Using a rubber hose attached to the faucet, first adjust the water temperature to a comfortably warm setting. Then gently wet the kitten down, starting from his neck and working down to the rump. Praise him while working the water into the coat. Next, gently wet his head, using your cupped hand instead of the hose. Then work a small amount of vet-approved cat shampoo into the coat until a good lather is built up. Be casual and fast, while praising the kitten the entire time. Be careful not to get shampoo into his eyes. Then, quickly and thoroughly rinse him off, taking care not to leave any soap residue. Dry him off completely with a clean, soft towel, then reward him with his favorite treat. Try to bathe the kitten at least once a month, even if it means just using plain water, to keep him conditioned to the procedure. If at any time the cat becomes highly agitated or aggressive, however, end the practice and let a professional groomer take over. It's not worth losing his trust over a few measly fleas.

BEGGING

DESCRIPTION

When your cat makes a pest out of himself every time you are either preparing food or actually eating, you can be pretty sure he is begging for a handout. He will meow, rub against you, and perhaps even paw at you, all in an effort to get you to surrender a morsel of food. Some cats will jump right up onto the counter or dinner table in an effort to score a tasty treat.

WHY YOUR CAT IS DOING THIS

Several factors could be causing your cat to beg incessantly. First, you may be underfeeding her. An underfed cat will out of necessity try to find more to eat and may resort to begging. Most owners feed their cats enough, however, and can tell if their pets are underweight simply by looking and feeling. If you are in doubt, though, consult your veterinarian, who will determine an ideal weight for your cat. Then all you need do is weigh her once a month to determine if she is at her ideal weight. If she is, you know she is begging for other reasons.

If your cat was once a stray or shelter cat, she may have had to at one time struggle to get food. If this is so, she might retain a very high food drive for much of her life, which could precipitate the begging behavior.

The most common cause of begging behavior in a cat, though, comes from the actions of the owner, who may have gotten into the habit of too often giving his or her cat treats and leftovers throughout the day. By doing so the well-meaning owner conditions his or her cat to beg.

SOLUTION

To minimize begging behavior in your cat, try the following:

1. Make sure your cat is at her proper weight to ensure she is getting enough food.
2. Feed her on a regular schedule instead of free-feeding all day. By doing so you will be able to teach the cat that she gets to eat at a prescribed time each day, instead of at any time. Her hunger pangs will peak right at feeding time, instead of at random times during the day.
3. Give her treats only when you are trying to encourage a particular behavior. If you feed her random treats throughout the day, you will condition her to beg for more.
4. Never feed your cat from your dinner plate. Also, do not feed her food intended for human consumption.

5. Never give your cat food while you are preparing a meal at the kitchen counter. If you choose to give her something, place it in her food dish instead.

If your cat continues to jump up onto the table or the kitchen counter in an effort to beg, simply keep a spray bottle filled with water handy. When she jumps up, give her a spritz while saying, "No!" She will quickly get the idea.

BITING

DESCRIPTION

Not to be confused with outright aggressive behavior (see previous section), unpredictable biting by a seemingly well adjusted cat can be upsetting and puzzling to an owner. The cat is sitting in your lap in a relaxed manner getting petted and stroked; she purrs softly, obviously enjoying the attention. Then, without warning, she reaches her head back and bites you, not hard enough to break the skin but enough for it to hurt. You let her go, wondering what you did wrong. Afterward, she acts as if nothing happened, perhaps even coming back for more petting.

WHY YOUR CAT IS DOING THIS

A number of reasons exist for this seemingly confusing behavior. Some cats will simply reach a saturation point with regard to handling; a quick bite is used as a signal for you to end the behavior. This type of behavior is especially common among unneutered cats, as well as those who have spent a great deal of time outdoors and have had to deal with the physical attentions of other cats.

If your cat is insecure, she may also exhibit this type of behavior. She enjoys the petting and stroking but may feel uncomfortable with too long a session. A quick, light bite is her way of ending the session without making too much of a scene.

Remember also that cats are by nature quite solitary and do not experience much physical contact in the wild, save at mating time. The physical contact experienced at that time isn't exactly enjoyable, either, especially for the female, who is bitten and held by the neck and then subjected to a painful bout of intercourse with the male. For this reason, many unneutered females (especially those who have mated or are in heat) will not enjoy too much petting and handling about the neck without eventually reacting to it. For whatever reason, many cats will reach a tolerance level at some point and then endure the petting no longer, even if it feels good. When that happens, the cat will give a light bite to say "enough."

Cats who have been roughhoused with since kittenhood may be more likely to bite, thinking that the behavior is simply part of the playing process. In additional, kittens, used to playing hard with their littermates, will often bite, thinking it a part of socializing. Often this behavior transfers over to the owner, who can be seen as a littermate by the playful, boisterous cat.

Some cats bite upon being petted simply because they don't like where they are being touched. The neck and the rump of the cat are two extremely sensitive areas; most cats will tolerate being handled at these areas for a short time only. Linger too long (especially at the rump), and your cat may warn you to quit with a small bite.

SOLUTION

If your cat is already exhibiting some type of biting behavior, you should:

1. Limit petting and grooming sessions to under a minute. The idea is to stop any type of physical contact before she reaches her saturation point. Keep her wanting to come back for more; avoid letting her make the decision to stop.
2. Pay attention to your cat's body language while petting her. If you see her tail begin to thrash back and forth or feel her body tense up, end the touching session.
3. Consider giving your cat a small tasty treat after each short handling session. This will stop her from worrying about being touched and focus her attentions and thoughts on the reward to come.

To prevent the biting behavior from surfacing in the first place, you should:

1. Get your cat neutered before she reaches sexual maturity.
2. Keep your cat indoors, which will prevent hostile interactions with other cats. Many well-adjusted house cats learn to play rough and bite from these interactions.
3. Socialize, handle, and groom your cat from as early on as possible, to desensitize her to touch.
4. Allow your cat plenty of time to herself.
5. Let your cat decide when she wants to be petted.
6. Don't allow petting sessions to go on for too long; end them while she is still enjoying herself.
7. Make sure your cat has no hidden injuries by taking her to the veterinarian on a regular basis.

CAR SICKNESS

DESCRIPTION

Though rarer in cats than dogs, car sickness does afflict some felines. Your carsick cat may vocalize quite a bit and may also vomit. On subsequent trips, he may show a real aversion to getting into the car or travel crate.

WHY YOUR CAT IS DOING THIS

Motion sickness is relatively rare in cats, due to the unique structure of the feline inner ear. Designed to give the cat an unparalleled sense of balance under almost any circumstance, this marvelous structure gives the cat the ability to leap, twist, and fly through the air without losing any sense of balance or direction. This anatomical structure makes it nearly impossible for a healthy cat to suffer from car sickness, which involves very subtle and regular motions, mild in comparison to what the cat is used to.

A cat suffering from an inner ear infection, however, may have the balancing mechanism thrown askew, making it possible for car sickness to occur.

SOLUTION

If your cat shows any signs of car sickness, your first step should be to take him to the veterinarian, who will inspect his ears carefully. The veterinarian will look for wax buildup, parasitic infection, and any type of viral or bacterial infection that could affect the cat's ability to regulate his balance mechanism. A thorough cleaning or a round of antibiotics will most likely clear up the problem quickly, solving the motion sickness dilemma.

You can help prevent ear infections in your cat by inspecting his ears on a regular basis. Look for any parasites, including fleas, ticks, and mites. Also, check for waxy buildup and dirt. If you start in early kittenhood, you should be able to clean your cat's ears yourself, using a cotton swab dipped in mineral oil. Don't probe too deep, however, and do make the cleaning session as fast as possible, rewarding the cat afterward with a treat. If your cat won't allow the procedure, let your veterinarian or groomer do it for you.

CHEWING

DESCRIPTION

Normally a habit of kittens in the teething stage, chewing on an appropriate, veterinarian-approved chew toy is an acceptable habit that needs to be performed until the cat's permanent teeth come in. Unfortunately, kittens will often chew on anything handy, including valuable items in the home and electrical wiring. The kitten will find something with just the right texture and chew on it avidly. Some adult cats never quite outgrow the chewing habit, to the chagrin of the owners, who often have to replace destroyed items in the home.

WHY YOUR CAT IS DOING THIS

Teething kittens need to chew to relieve the discomfort of teething. If no specific chew toys are provided for them, they will select some item in the home to gnaw on. Often this can be wiring, clothing, or even furniture. In the case of wiring, this habit could cause the death of the pet. Adult cats rarely present owners with a chewing problem unless they have for some reason not outgrown the behavior or have some ongoing dental or gum problem whose pain is relieved by chewing.

SOLUTION

All kittens should be provided with a few safe chew toys during the day to satisfy the need to chew. The toys can be made of yarnlike material or any kind of thick, durable floss fabric that feels good in the kitten's mouth. Make sure the toys do not have buttons or other pieces that can break off and choke the pet. To get your kitten interested, introduce the toy by teasing her with it, to invoke her prey drive instincts. Scoot the toy around on the floor back and forth in front of the kitten; tease her with it until she wants it badly, then let her have it. You might even consider smearing a small amount of tuna juice onto a portion of the toy to get the kitten really excited. Then just let her chew on it to her heart's content.

At the same time, you need to discourage the kitten from chewing on items that either have value to you or might potentially hurt her. Make sure to hide all wires under the carpeting or else tape them down securely with duct tape. With wires such as the telephone cord, which needs to be out in the open, try spraying them down every so often with a repellent such as Bitter Apple spray. You can also wipe them down with a soap-and-water mixture, which tastes very bitter to the cat. If the problem is severe, try applying hot mustard or hot sauce to exposed wires or any other chewed-on item. The kitten should get the message. Adult cats who have never lost the chewing desire should be treated in the same manner.

In addition, when you catch your cat or kitten in the act of chewing on a forbidden item, give her a quick spray with some water (while simultaneously saying, *"No"!*). Do not, however, hit the cat or throw anything at her.

CHEWING, FABRIC AND CLOTHING

DESCRIPTION

Interestingly, some felines, especially Siamese and mixed-Siamese cats, develop a desire to chew and suck on wool and wool-like fabrics. Blankets, sweaters, socks, and balls of yarn are sought out, especially clothing that has significant human scent on it. The cat chews and suckles on the fabric, often rendering the piece of clothing unwearable.

WHY YOUR CAT IS DOING THIS

Cats weaned at too early an age will often try to suckle on people, other animals, and even articles of clothing. A cat who has a penchant for suckling and chewing on your clothes may be expressing this unusual need. The cat in question often seeks out the articles of clothing that have the most scent, such as socks, underwear, and the underarms of shirts or sweaters, possibly because these areas remind your pet of you (her foster parent). This unusual habit can end up costing you a tidy sum, especially if a few good sweaters are ruined.

SOLUTION

The first step in trying to stop this expensive behavior is removing all chewable articles of clothing from the cat's domain. Instead of keeping sweaters on open shelves, put them in drawers or closed closets. Do the same with all clothing or blankets, and refrain from leaving used articles of clothing out for the cat to find.

Next, provide your cat with a soft, stuffed toy that she can chew on to her heart's content. Handle the toy often, to get your scent on it. Hopefully this will give her an acceptable outlet for her chewing/suckling habit.

If the problem is severe, you may need to set your

cat up. Take a few old articles of clothing and soak them in a sink filled with soapy water. Then remove and dry them, without rinsing the soap out. Next, leave them out for your cat to find. If she begins to chew or suckle on them, she will quickly get the bitter soapy taste in her mouth, causing her to abruptly end the behavior. Trying this for a week or so should minimize the behavior, especially if you have provided her with a soft stuffed toy to chew on.

When choosing a kitten, try to determined at what age the litter was weaned. Kittens weaned before the seventh or eighth week will have a greater chance of exhibiting this fabric-chewing behavior.

CLIMBING, ON DRAPERY

DESCRIPTION

A good number of cats enjoy climbing up the drapes, usually a habit that begins during kittenhood. They will most often be in an excited or playful mood and simply leap onto the drapery, climb up to the top, and then survey their "kingdoms." Unfortunately, drapes can be ruined quickly by these feline climbers.

WHY YOUR CAT IS DOING THIS

Cats love to get up as high as possible, to survey their territories or to find a spot where no one can disturb them. Many cats also can become bored at home and will begin climbing the drapes out of a need to release pent-up energies.

SOLUTION

If your kitten or cat is climbing the drapes, the first thing to do is attempt to make them inaccessible to the pet. Switch to a style that ends higher up on the wall, or else tie a knot in each drape. Also try placing doubled-sided transparent tape down on the flooring at the base of the drapes, in an attempt to keep the cat from walking up to a good "launching site."

If you catch your cat in the act, spray him with water while saying *"No!"* He should leap off of the drapes at that point, if he doesn't want to keep getting drenched. Each time he begins to climb up the drapes, squirt him. Eventually he will begin to think twice about it.

Next, go out and purchase a multitiered "kitty condo" from your local pet shop. Usually five-to-seven-foot-high, carpeted structures, these play structures have several platforms and resting stations that will amuse your cat and help get him off the floor and into an elevated position. Odds are he will completely forget about the drapes. If you do purchase the kitty condo, be sure to frequently place a few treats up on the top levels to encourage him to go up there as often as possible.

In addition, be sure to exercise your cat to help relieve his boredom. Get out a teaser toy or a yarn ball and have a go at it; get him to chase the toy around. Really stimulate his prey instincts. Throw the ball up a flight of stairs, and see if you can get him to chase up after it. Getting him moving and thinking will help relieve his boredom and get his mind off of the drapes.

CLIMBING, ON PEOPLE

DESCRIPTION

You are walking through your home, perhaps on the way to watch some television. All of a sudden your tabby kitten is shimmying her way up your leg, her sharp little claws tearing through your clothing and digging into your skin. Kittens especially are known for this behavior, though adult cats not taught to cease the behavior will exhibit it as well.

WHY YOUR CAT IS DOING THIS

Young kittens have to interact with their littermates in order to learn acceptable and unacceptable behavior. If kittens get too rough with another, they will be either swatted or jumped on or else be made to hear the cries of the hurt sibling. Either way, kittens learn how to modulate their behavior according to what is or is not acceptable.

If your kitten was unfortunate enough to leave his litter at too early an age (before eight weeks), odds are he might not have had sufficient time to learn proper social skills and may not know that climbing up someone's leg is unacceptable behavior. The little guy just never learned good manners.

Other cats will climb up a person's leg to get some attention or to possibly get at a piece of food the person might be holding. This is also bad manners, and such cats have a dominant mind-set that may need adjustment.

SOLUTION

If your kitten or cat has a habit of trying to climb up your body, the first thing to do is wear clothing that will protect you from those sharp claws and not get ruined in the process. If the offender is a young kitten, you can grasp him by the scruff, pull him off you, and then hold him up and say, *"No!"* in a firm tone. Then put him down and ignore him for a few minutes. If your adult cat is climbing up your body, don't try the same scruff technique, as the cat may overreact and scratch you. Instead, begin jumping up and down briskly, while at the same saying, *"No!"* in a loud voice, repeatedly. He will immediately jump off you and think you've popped a cork. If you do this every time the cat tries to climb up your body, odds are he will soon stop the annoying behavior.

COPROPHAGY, OR STOOL EATING

DESCRIPTION

Though much less common in cats than dogs, coprophagy can occur in cats as well, particularly outdoor cats, who are exposed to the feces of various species and to feces not covered with cat litter, surely a most unappetizing substance. The cat in question, much to the owner's dismay, will simply consume small quantities of stool at various times, with no predictable frequency.

WHY YOUR CAT IS DOING THIS

Though it is often hard to completely understand why a cat might choose to consume feces, several explanations come to mind. First, the feces of some animals may actually give off an appetizing aroma to the cat, due perhaps to additives that may have been in the food eaten by the originator of the stool in question. Or your stool-eating cat might be suffering from a dietary deficiency of some sort and somehow trying to supplement his diet to alleviate the problem. A cat who once spent time as a stray might also have developed the habit, as feces contain very small amounts of nutrients and might have been at times all that the cat could find to eat.

SOLUTION

If your cat spends time outdoors and is eating the stool of other animals, there is little you can do to stop the behavior, as most of the time you won't be present when the act occurs. The only sure way to stop your cat from eating feces outside is keeping him indoors. An indoor cat won't have access to feces that are not encrusted with cat litter and so won't in all likelihood continue the habit. You could try to modify the behavior by lacing some stool with hot sauce, then leaving it in an easily found spot. Doing so several times might just cure your cat of this disgusting habit.

If keeping your cat indoors is not an option for you, the next step is to determine if, in fact, your cat is suffering from some dietary deficiency, causing him to eat feces. To do this, you will need to have your veterinarian run some tests to determine if your cat is low in some essential nutrient such as taurine, fiber, or some necessary vitamin or mineral.

The only other measure you can take to prevent the habit is keeping your property as free from animal stool as possible. Keep your cat's litter box well scooped, even though rare cats will consume their own litter-encrusted stool.

DEPRESSION

DESCRIPTION

Cats suffering from depression often show a marked reduction in activity and may not be as diligent about taking care of their hygiene as often as they once were. Appetite may decline, and elimination habits may suffer as well. In addition, the depressed cat may vocalize and sleep more than a well-adjusted animal.

Recognizing depression in a cat can be quite difficult, as its symptoms can closely mirror those of any number of physical ailments. Only after a visit to the veterinarian has ruled out any medical abnormalities can the diagnosis of depression be verified.

WHY YOUR CAT IS DOING THIS

The list of causes for feline depression is as long as that for human depression. Almost anything could cause your cat to fall into a depressive funk. It really depends on the cat. Several factors, however, are often to blame for a cat falling into a prolonged depression. These include:

Loss of another pet or person in the household. Because your cat can become as emotionally attached to another pet or person as you, the removal of that individual from your cat's life can be a traumatic and depressing experience, and one that can take a long time for the cat to get over.

Change of environment. Moving to another home can worry and depress a cat, who becomes very attached to a "territory" and stressed at its sudden loss. Changing an outdoor cat over to an indoor-only environment can also temporarily cause your cat to become sullen and irritable.

Change within the environment. Often a change of home decor (such as new furniture or carpets) can set your cat off and cause her to lament. Suddenly closing her out of your bedroom at night can hurt her feelings. Even the disappearance of a favorite toy or litter box can often depress a cat for a prolonged period of time. The addition of any strange new sights, sounds, or scents might also throw your sweet cat for an emotional loop.

Change in food or litter. Often something as seemingly trivial (to us) as a change in one or both of these cat staples can throw a cat for an emotional loop.

Change of schedule. Doing things differently or at a different time can alter a cat's mood substantially. For instance, if you change to a night shift at your job and are suddenly gone all night long, your cat could become stressed and sullen. Feeding your cat at a different time of day or even having a regular visitor suddenly start showing up at a different time of the day can upset some cats.

Boredom. If your cat has very little stimuli in her world she can eventually become depressed and lethargic. Reducing or removing a familiar activity in the cat's life can also depress her.

Lack of exercise. As is the case with boredom, any cat who gets little or no exercise each day can eventually become moody and depressed.

SOLUTION

The very first step in trying to solve your cat's depression is taking her to your veterinarian, who will examine her thoroughly to determine if an injury or other physical disorder is causing her depression. Remember that cats tend to be stoic about pain and illness; the only sign could closely resemble depression.

If physical discomfort has been ruled out, the next step is thinking carefully about your cat's environment. Has it changed at all in the last few weeks? Think about anything that might have changed in her life, even if it was something as seemingly trivial as a stinky old toy being thrown away.

Once you come up with a list of changes, attempt to reverse as many of them as possible. Pull that toy out of the garbage. Switch back to that old brand of food or litter. Move the furniture back the way it was. Whatever is fixable fix. Move the food dish or litter box back to where it was. Put the same old talk show back on the radio while you are away. Whatever you can think of, try to return the status quo.

If you think the loss of a pet might be the cause, think twice before replacing the animal right away.

Though the loss might in fact be causing your cat's depression, getting a new cat might backfire, causing your older cat to feel threatened. It's best to wait a while before replacing a lost pet, to see if your current cat learns to adjust to the new situation. Instead, consider adding some new toys and props to her world. Put a newspaper-filled box in the living room or buy a new scratching post. Sometimes a new distraction can help relieve the pain of loss. If the depression is being caused by the departure of a person from the home, see if you can arrange for him or her to visit your cat every so often, to help assuage her feelings of loss.

If you have changed the cat's schedule somehow, attempt to return to the old way, if possible. If you are now working a different schedule, see if a person your cat knows well can come over for a few minutes while you are gone to keep her company. Often this is enough to pull a sullen cat out of the doldrums.

If your cat is depressed due to boredom, try adding some fun to her life. Get her new toys. Buy a "kitty condo." Hide treats around the home for her to discover. Get her chasing a "teaser toy" around the house. Play a pet video on the television. Leave an ice cube in her dish. Whatever you can come up with that interests her will suffice.

If you suspect that your cat is depressed due to now being denied access to the outdoors, try to make her new indoor territory as interesting as possible by following the suggestions for boredom. In addition, consider keeping a shade up on one window, allowing her to look out on the yard or street out front. If this causes her to meow incessantly, however, close the shade and try to increase the fun factor in the home.

Last, get your cat moving around more. This applies particularly to indoor-only cats, who get less exercise and stimuli than their outdoor cousins. Play with your cat to get her heart pumping. Throw a ball or a catnip-filled yarn toy around. Move her food dish to the top of a flight of stairs to get her running up and down them. Whatever you can do to get her moving around will help.

Most of all, before making major changes in your home or lifestyle consider how they will affect your cat. If you can't avoid changing something, try to do so as gradually as possible, to acclimate her to the new situation.

Some owners of depressed cats have helped moderate their cats' depression through the use of veterinarian-approved prescription drugs. Numerous mood-altering medications exist that can have the same antidepressant effects on cats as Prozac or tricyclic drugs have on humans. If your cat's depression hasn't responded to any environmental changes you have made, consider discussing this option with your veterinarian.

DESTRUCTIVE BEHAVIOR

DESCRIPTION

Though causing destruction of property in and around the home is much more common in dogs, cats, too, have the potential for this behavior. More likely to be exhibited by kittens and adolescent cats than by older pets, typical results of destructive behavior are torn-up newspapers, damaged furniture, overturned book-shelves, counters in disarray, clothing dragged or deposited in random places, gardens destroyed, pictures knocked off walls, and overturned houseplants. (Damaged furniture, particularly sofas or chairs found scratched and clawed apart, will be addressed in a separate listing, "Scratching Furniture."

WHY YOUR CAT IS DOING THIS

Several factors can be responsible for your cat (or cats) causing random damage to your home. First, your unneutered cat might be feeling the need to get out of the home and mate but cannot, at least when kept as an indoor pet. So, in response to his frustration, the cat may let it out by ripping things up or knocking things over. Or you may simply have a frisky kitten or young cat with lots of energy to burn and plenty of high jinks up his sleeve. Two young cats together, while playing or chasing each other around the home, can get into all manner of trouble, spilling and toppling and overturning everything in sight. In addition, your cat may simply become so bored in a nonstimulating environment that he acts out, destroying things as a means of voicing his frustrations. Whatever the cause, this cat has not yet learned what you deem to be proper and improper behavior, probably because you have not taught him what behaviors are acceptable or unacceptable.

SOLUTION

The first step in minimizing destructive behavior in the home is having your cat neutered. Doing so will remove the mating drive and all the nonthinking mayhem that can arise from it. This will work on adult cats as well, though it may take as long as several months for the behavior to stop, as the hormone levels responsible for the behavior take time to wane.

Next, you must make your home as cat-proof as possible. Do not leave food or dirty dishes on counters or newspapers on the coffee table or chair. Place houseplants in suspended hangers or secure them into position with wall anchors and picture frame wires, so the cat can't knock them over. Cover the tops of the pots with round plastic covers (available at department stores and garden supply stores) to prevent your cat from spilling soil onto the flooring. Also, pick up after yourself; avoid leaving clothing scattered about, as your cat might decide to drag it around the home for hours or chew it to shreds.

Perhaps the most effective way to minimize destructive behavior in your cat is to create for her an environment filled with interesting things to do. Place fun cat toys down on the floor. Buy your cat a "kitty condo" with several carpeted platforms, levels, and enclosures, as well as a base column that doubles as a scratching post. Put down a cardboard box filled with shredded newspaper and a few treats. Leave a few treats down in random places for your cat to find. Move her food dish around. Leave a radio playing softly, tuned in to talk radio. The more you do to make your cat's world more interesting, the less you will have to deal with destructive behavior.

Destructive behavior rarely occurs while you are right there. If it does, however, feel free to correct your cat by spraying her with water from a spray bottle and saying, *"No!"* Do not, however, hit her or throw any objects at her, as this could traumatize the cat and cause more behavior problems.

DIGGING, INTO FLOWER BEDS OR POTTED PLANTS

DESCRIPTION

The cat with a penchant for digging will often do so in a well-turned and tended garden or (in the case of an indoor-only cat) in the rich soil of one or more of your prized potted plants. The plant or crop in question is often pulled up and destroyed, and cat stool is deposited where you least want it to be.

WHY YOUR CAT IS DOING THIS

Cats have been digging into earth for many thousands of years in order to bury their feces and urine, so as not to alert possible predators to their location. Some cats also bury waste materials so as not to provoke a territorial squabble with a neighbor cat, who may be the clearly dominant animal. Your cat has the instinct to bury his waste, too, and will do it every day of his life. Most cat owners are aware of this; even eight-week-old kittens have litter box usage down pat.

If you allow your cat regular access to the outdoors, he will eventually begin digging and eliminating in certain areas around your property. Flower beds are a prime location for this, as the earth there is often softer and easier to move than firmer soil found elsewhere. Cats will also choose to dig and eliminate in sandboxes, if available. This behavior is normal and shouldn't surprise you at all.

Your indoor cat who chooses to dig up (and possibly eliminate in) the soil of a houseplant is obeying the same instinct as his outdoor brethren. The difference, however, is that he does have a better alternative available, namely, a litter box. He may be using the box and also choosing to use the plant, or he may be ignoring the box completely. A cat who prefers digging and eliminating into a houseplant instead of his litter box probably does not like something about the box and is looking for an alternative spot inside the home. The litter box might not be properly scooped, or the brand of litter may not be to his liking. Or competition with other cats in the home may cause him to search out his own place to eliminate, one that has less traffic and less of a chance for confrontation.

SOLUTION

Stopping your cat from digging up your flower beds outside is a difficult task indeed, especially if you allow your cat to stay outside all day. Gardening supply stores do sell plastic or metal meshing that can be placed atop open soil, making digging difficult or impossible. Your cat has to eliminate somewhere, however; odds are he will find a spot to do so. The first way to prevent him from destroying your garden or flower beds is to simply bring him indoors on a full-time basis, making sure that he has a clean litter box available at all times. He will be safer indoors and will live a longer, healthier life as well. If you simply can't deny him access to the outdoors, try placing several litter boxes around the property in hopes that he might use them instead of the garden. If you do so, though, other neighborhood cats may take liberties in them as well. Also, if you have a dog, he will find the cat stools in the litter box and happily eat them (a disgusting habit but common nonetheless). Consider building an enclosed structure, similar to a fenced-in dog run, and allowing your cat to have access to it for several hours each day. Place a litter box inside it and perhaps a water and food dish. Be sure to close in the top as well, as cats can climb quite well, thank you. By constructing this "cat run" you will be giving your feline access to the outdoors without many of the inherent risks. Other cats (or dogs) won't be able to hurt or infect him, he won't get lost or run over, and he won't be able to ruin your nice plantings.

If your indoor cat is digging into the soil of your plants (and possibly eliminating in them), try scooping the cat's litter box more often. If the problem began just around the time you switched brands of cat litter, consider going back to the original brand. Your cat might not like the feel or scent of the new litter and be searching for alternative spots to eliminate. If you have two or more cats, try introducing a second or even a third litter box. Often one cat will not like sharing a litter box, especially with cats he or she doesn't like or is afraid of.

Last, go to your garden supply store or pet shop and purchase plastic flower pot covers, designed to deny cats access to the soil. These covers have holes in the middle big enough to let the plant grow through. They are easily removable, allowing you to water whenever necessary. This should put a stop to your cat's unwanted digging.

DROOLING

DESCRIPTION

Some cats develop a habit of drooling at certain times during the day. Saliva will slowly drip from the cat's mouth and onto the hair below, creating a darkened wet area, more evident in longhaired breeds than in short-. The cat has no way of preventing this, as the feline's lips don't have the same ability as our own to hold in excess saliva.

WHY YOUR CAT IS DOING THIS

Cats suffering from some type of tooth or gum problem may begin to drool, due to the possibility that they cannot close their mouths entirely. A broken tooth, abscess, or oral infection can be quite painful and would easily cause the cat to pant and drool due to stress.

Certain diseases can cause a cat to drool. Rabies, distemper, and other infectious disorders can all have drooling as a side effect, all the more reason for bringing your cat to the veterinarian as soon as possible.

Some cats learn to drool whenever dinnertime approaches, especially if the smell of food is in the air for long periods of time. This is a natural response of cats, dogs, and many other mammals, including ourselves.

Other cats drool whenever they are being petted, a response to the relaxed, pleasant mood gentle stroking can bring on. Even sleeping cats can drool on occasion, especially if they are older.

SOLUTION

First, take your drooling cat to the veterinarian, who will examine her thoroughly for signs of gum or tooth disease or a possible abscess in the making. He or she will also attempt to rule out the chance of your cat having any type of infectious disease that could be causing the problem.

If your cat is given a clean bill of health, you must then assume that the drooling is a behavioral response to something in her environment. If the drooling occurs while you are preparing your own dinner, try feeding her just as you begin to cook, instead of during or after. Feeding her in a room other than the kitchen might help also. Consider feeding her two or three times a day instead of once to minimize her hunger pangs. Also, avoid giving her human food, as this will train her to drool whenever you eat something. Consider having a time during the day when you teach the cat some new behavior and reward her with a treat or two. This will keep her mind active and not so focused on dinnertime and will also help curb her hunger somewhat.

If your cat drools in response to petting, there is not much you can do. After all, you do not want to reduce desired physical contact, and you wouldn't want to deny her the pleasure of being stroked. Just clean up the excess, and be happy that she likes you.

The same goes for sleeping cats who drool. The fact that they are asleep makes behavioral modification impossible. Just put down some type of absorbent cloth down atop your drooling cat's sleeping spot and tell your friends not to laugh.

EATING TOXIC SUBSTANCES AND OBJECTS

DESCRIPTION

A cat who has ingested a toxic substance may quickly go into shock or experience seizures, convulsions, and loss of muscular control, followed by respiratory failure, paralysis, and death. The cat may also have accelerated respiration and heartbeat, dizziness, and dilated pupils. Some less toxic substances may render the cat sleepy or lethargic, or irritable and hyperactive. Many toxins will cause the cat to vomit and/or drool, with diarrhea and excess urination also possible.

WHY YOUR CAT IS DOING THIS

Your cat does not know how lethal certain household substances can be. She depends on you to keep them out of her environment. Some toxins (such as antifreeze, certain fertilizers, and cough syrup) may actually taste good to a cat and are therefore readily ingested. If potentially lethal substances are left out in the open, your cat will eventually find them and investigate. Kittens and young cats are especially prone to poisoning, due to their incredibly curious minds.

SOLUTION

The first step in preventing your cat from being poisoned is knowing what substances can harm her. These include:

- Acetaminophen
- Acid
- Alcohol
- Antifreeze
- Aspirin
- Battery acid
- Chlorine bleach
- Drain cleaner
- Fertilizer
- Gasoline or diesel fuel
- Household cleaners such as Windex, Lysol, and Mr. Clean
- Insecticides
- Motor oil
- Paint
- Prescription drugs
- Rat poison
- Solvents, such as paint thinner, rust remover, and tarnish remover

In addition, many types of house- and garden plants are toxic to cats. These are covered in the section titled "Plant Eating."

Get all of these substances out of your cat's environment and in securely locked cupboards, preferably located high up in the garage. Remember that cats are quite curious and adept at getting into impossible places, so be sure to take this into account. If your cat has access to the outdoors, you must be careful about putting fertilizer down on gardens and lawns, as she will spend a good amount of time digging and frolicking all over these areas. Rather than choosing a chemical fertilizer, consider using an organic alternative such as manure, especially for the garden, as it will be safe for the cat to be in contact with. Clean up all oil spills, particularly those on the driveway, in the garage, and on the street, as contact with oil can make your cat ill. Above all, *make sure that no antifreeze is left on the floor, driveway, or street*, as it is highly toxic and can kill your cat if ingested. Antifreeze has a sweet taste that dogs and cats love, so beware.

Keep all over-the-counter and prescription drugs stored away safely. Many cats can open medicine cabinets, so beware. Consider not keeping household cleaners under the kitchen or bathroom sinks, either, as many cats can easily open these with a flick of a paw.

If your cat has ingested a poisonous substance, you may need to act quickly to save her life. The common treatment is to induce vomiting, unless the poison consumed is of a corrosive nature, such as battery acid, fertilizer, or drain cleaner. Allowing these to come back up will further damage the cat's esophagus and oral cavity. Also avoid inducing vomiting if the cat is having convulsions or is losing consciousness.

To induce vomiting, administer two or three teaspoons of syrup of ipecac. If this is not available, get as much heavily salted water into the cat as possible. After she has vomited, get her to drink as much water or milk as possible. Force-feed her with a turkey baster if necessary. Then get her to the veterinarian as soon as possible. Also, discuss poisoning with your veterinarian in advance, as a precautionary measure.

Be sure to have an emergency telephone number for your veterinarian at the ready or the listing for a twenty-four-hour clinic. Also, you can call the *National Animal Poison Information Center* at 1-800-548-2423 for expert advice on what to do if your cat has ingested a toxic substance. If all else fails, try 911; someone there may be able to help. Whatever you do, get your cat to a veterinarian as quickly as you can.

Prevention by removal is the only effective way to dissuade your cat from eating toxic substances, as modifying the behavior requires her to actually perform the undesired act at least once or twice and then receive some form of negative reinforcement. It goes without saying that you do not want her to ever perform this undesired act; just one lick at some poisons could be fatal. So it is up to you to prevent this behavior from occurring by removing all toxins from the cat's world.

ESCAPING

DESCRIPTION

Escape is mostly a concern of those who own indoor-only cats, as some of these pets, unfortunately, find a way out of the home and out into an alien territory, namely, the outdoors. The escape is usually made through an open window or door and less often from an automobile during a time when the cat is being transported. Outdoor cats, especially those who have not been neutered, can also wander too far from home and "escape" from their familiar territories.

WHY YOUR CAT IS DOING THIS

Cats are curious animals with excellent senses that can sometimes get them into trouble. An open window and a flittering bird on the lawn outside is often all it takes to lure your cat out into what may be a very alien environment. Leave the front door open for a minute or so, and even the most timid indoor cat is apt to at least investigate the strange new world beyond the front steps. Let your indoor-only cat get outside, however, and he might become disoriented, frightened, and lost. Not used to the unpredictable world out there, he could easily be injured or killed.

Cats allowed to venture out on a regular basis can roam beyond the boundaries of their known territories and become escapees, so to speak. This often occurs with unneutered males, who, upon catching the scent of a female in heat, can travel as far as several miles from home in an attempt to mate. By the time the cat finds the female, he may be too far from home to find his way back.

Outdoor cats whose owners move to new neighborhoods can become homesick for their old territories, and might decide to go looking for it. These cats escape from the new, strange territory, and search in vain for the old, becoming lost in the process. Those who escape death from automobiles or other animals often become adopted by other cat lovers, who usually have no way to contact the real owners, due to few cats having identification tags, or else get picked up animal control agencies, where they may be euthanized.

SOLUTION

The first step in preventing your cat from escaping and becoming lost is checking all possible escape routes out of the home, making sure that the cat has no way out. If a window needs to be opened, check that a secure screen without tears is in place. The same goes for all doors; if one needs to be open, have a secure screen door in place, one that doesn't take too long to close on its own. If transporting your cat in the car, do so using a pet carrier, to prevent him from leaping out at an inopportune time. Most cats do not like car travel and often become stressed by it;

give them an out, and they will take it. Prevent this by putting your cat in a secure pet carrier.

Children are a major cause of cat escapes. They unintentionally leave windows or doors open, allowing the cat a tempting avenue out. If you do have children, talk to them about closing all doors and windows to prevent kitty from getting outside.

The best way to prevent a cat from wandering away is to keep him inside all the time. An indoor cat is much less likely to wander or escape, providing all windows and doors are secure. If your cat is raised from kittenhood as an indoor-only cat, chances are he will not even want to venture outdoors for too long, as he considers it alien territory. His territory is the home, and that's where he will focus his time and attention.

If keeping your cat indoors doesn't appeal to you, you will need to somehow ensure he won't wander off too far from home. The simplest way of doing so is having the pet neutered. By doing so you will remove one of the biggest causes of cat disappearances. They don't call them strays for nothing. A neutered male won't have the desire to seek out that female in heat a mile away. A neutered female will not have any desire to seek out a mate. Also, neutering will prevent unwanted pregnancies, the biggest cause of cat deaths. If you ever had to witness an entire litter of unwanted kittens being euthanized, you would think twice about allowing your unneutered cat to breed indiscriminately.

If you do allow your cat access to the outdoors, be sure to place an identification tag on him. Attach it to a stretch collar, to prevent the cat from choking to death in the event the collar catches on something. Be sure to have your name and telephone number on the tag, along with the cat's name.

One way to prevent your cat from attempting an escape is to make sure he is not bored. See the listing titled "Destructive Behavior" for suggestions on how to relieve boredom. By following these suggestions you will divert much of his energy into his own territory and away from thoughts of escape.

EXCESSIVE PREY DRIVE

DESCRIPTION

Normally the venue of outdoor cats, predation on small animals by felines can often reach alarming proportions. Some cats will kill three or more rodents, birds, snakes, or fish every day; over a period of fifteen years that amounts to thousands of animals. Often an owner will come home to find one or more little "presents" at the front or back door, there perhaps to announce the pet's hunting acumen. Excessive prey drive is also possible with an indoor cat, as many homebound felines make the lives of other household pets miserable and more than a little frightening.

WHY YOUR CAT IS DOING THIS

No surprise here. Cats are predators and have been for millions of years. Many are very good at stalking and killing small things. Why expect your cat to be any different? If you allow your cat access to the outdoors, she may begin killing small creatures. Some cats are better at it than others, however, particularly rescued strays, who may have needed to survive on their hunting skills alone for long periods of time. If you have a rescued cat, odds are her prey drive will be high.

The same goes for indoor cats. If presented with the opportunity, most will attack and kill a small creature such as a hamster, parakeet, or goldfish. Again, if the indoor cat was once a stray, the chances of this happening are much higher.

SOLUTION

The easiest way to minimize your cat's predation on outdoor animals is to keep her indoors. Though your cat is a natural predator, she is being taken care of by you and no longer needs to kill. The birds and rodents outside shouldn't be trophies for a domesticated pet but rather food for a needy animal. Don't take pride in your cat's hunting abilities if the killings are not necessary. Your cat has a nice dish of food waiting inside every day; those little creatures have to fend for themselves.

If you insist on allowing your cat outdoors, attaching a small bell to her collar can be a great way of warning her prey that she is in the area. Though she can still practice her stalking, the number of kills should go down significantly.

If you own an indoor-only cat, consider not purchasing any small pets that she will consider prey. Avoid all rodents and birds (though some of the larger parrots can be quite intimidating to most cats), as these tend to be too vulnerable to a cat's hunting abilities. If you must have fish, be sure to locate the tank in an inaccessible area. Cover the tank with a sturdy top to prevent the fishing feline from dipping in with a paw and hooking a few.

If you must have rodents and/or birds, locate them in a part of the home that is permanently off-limits to the cat. Make sure any children present know to keep the cat out and the doors closed.

Though some cats, if raised with a small prey animal from early kittenhood, may tolerate and even befriend the creature, the risk of the natural hunting instincts coming to the surface at some time are probably greater than the bond between the two (especially if the cat has missed a meal).

EXCESSIVE VOCALIZATION

DESCRIPTION

For a variety of reasons, some cats will at certain times vocalize more than others. Whether it be a meow, squeak, chirp, scream, or howl, all felines are capable of a variety of vocalizations, depending on mood and circumstance. Though one person's definition of "excessive" may not agree with another's, most would agree that nonstop meowing, caterwauling, crying, or wailing is undesirable.

WHY YOUR CAT IS DOING THIS

Several reasons can explain why your cat is as vocal as he is. First, he may be of a breed that tends to vocalize more than others. If he is a Siamese, Burmese, or Tonkinese, odds are he will be very talkative, meowing and caterwauling all the time to get attention, express his happiness (or anxiety), or just comment on life in general. Abyssinians can also be quite talkative. This is normal behavior for these breeds; if you don't want a talkative cat, don't go near these four.

Excess vocalization could be a sign that your cat is in pain. Though most cats tend to internalize discomfort, some will express it through constant meowing or howling, often combined with pacing. If your cat shows these signs, take him to the veterinarian for a checkup, to eliminate illness or injury as a possibility.

A frequent cause of excess vocalization in a cat is the desire to mate. Females in heat will howl plaintively in an attempt to locate or attract a male. If your female cat is not neutered, expect her to wail away whenever her time comes, which, unlike the cycle in dogs, will occur all year long, with little break in between.

The actual mating act will also cause your female to howl and scream in pain. Unforgettably haunting sounds, the female's cries during coitus can sober even the most stoic of owners.

Some cats vocalize when emotionally stressed, particularly if moved from familiar surroundings or separated from a loved one or litter of kittens. Like ourselves, cats become attached to places, companions, and offspring; having any one of these suddenly taken away can cause a cat to meow or wail in lamentation.

SOLUTION

Eliminate the possibility of your cat being hurt or sick by visiting the veterinarian. He or she will check the cat for any signs of illness or injury, allowing you to explore other causes and solutions to the vocalization problem.

Consider having your female cat neutered. Doing so will remove the urge to mate, effectively halting the need to call out to males or scream in pain during intercourse.

If your cat is calling out because of a loss of territory, companionship, or kittens, there is not much you can do except pay attention to her and give her affection. Try to distract her with play, toys, and treats. Introduce new distractions, such as a cardboard box stuffed with newspaper or a "kitty condo." Do not, however, consider getting a new kitten at this point. The older cat's loss may actually be directed at the new pet in the form of redirected aggression. Instead, simply be there for her and let time heal the wounds. Be sure not to let your cat escape at this time, as she might wander far in search of whatever she has lost. If she is an outdoor cat, consider limiting her to the home for a while before allowing her outside again, to give her time to acclimate to the scents, sights, and sounds of the new home.

~

FEAR OF LOUD NOISES

DESCRIPTION

Though most cats tend to shy away from loud, unexpected noises, some are more upset by them than others. Your timid or nervous cat will certainly dislike any overly loud noises such as the sounds of construction work, blaring car horns, and loud music. She will most likely run off and hide in the part of the home farthest from the commotion. In severe cases, your cat might panic and try to escape the home or even attack someone trying to comfort her. These cats often exhibit secondary behavioral problems, such as loss of appetite, irregular house-training habits, and possible fear aggression.

WHY YOUR CAT IS DOING THIS

Shying away from a very loud, unexpected noise is a completely normal reaction for any cat to have. Any sudden occurrence such as this could mean danger;

running away is simply a normal reaction to a perceived threat. Firecrackers, cars backfiring, extremely loud music, boisterous clapping or yelling, and thunder are all sounds that you should expect your cat to react to. Accordingly, you should do all you can to eliminate as many of these upsetting experiences from her life as possible.

Some timid or nervous cats, however, have a much lower threshold to noise than do well-adjusted pets. The sound of a car horn down the block, for instance, normally taken in stride by the average cat, could send the sensitive cat running for the hills. A loud conversation, boisterous laughter, or a rock song on the radio can all set your fearful, timid cat off, sending her to her favorite hiding place for the remainder of the day. She senses the disturbance as a threat to her wellbeing, causing her to seek out safety. Try to pick her up during this time and you could get scratched or bitten.

Some cats simply have a low tolerance to noise. Those raised in quiet surroundings, then suddenly brought to a noisy environment could react badly to all the commotion going on, sounds that we take for granted. Other cats, timid by nature, simply won't tolerate unpredictable noise and will spend much of their time hiding and skulking. Still others might have experienced a loud, traumatic event during kittenhood; the fear of the episode imprints upon them and stays with them throughout their adult lives. Any reminder of the event can send them into a panic.

SOLUTION

The first step in dealing with this problem is ensuring that as few loud noises as possible invade your cat's environment. Never allow anyone to explode firecrackers on your property or play music at maximum volume. Instruct all children not to yell and scream while at your home, out of consideration for the cat. Keep home construction projects down to a minimum; if one is unavoidable, try to complete it as quickly as possible. During that time, consider allowing your cat to visit a friend's home, making sure that she is kept indoors only, to prevent the temporary change in territory from causing her to run away. If street sounds tend to be on the loud side, invest in a good set of drapes for the windows, which will help muffle the sounds. Keep the windows closed, too, unless your home becomes too warm. Consider double-pane, soundproof windows also. If possible, house the cat in the part of the home farthest from the street noise.

Slowly desensitizing your cat to slightly higher volumes of sound can help lower her stress levels. Begin doing so by playing the radio or television while you are away. Start out with the volume adjusted very low, then slowly increase it over a few weeks' time until it is set at a normal level, one that you might use for everyday listening. Also try randomly clapping your hands during the day, softly at first, then incrementally louder, until your cat seems to be able to tolerate the sound without panicking. Throughout this exercise provide your cat with treat rewards and lots of praise. You can even walk around the home singing at varying volumes (but only if you have a voice that does not upset your cat further). Throughout any noise desensitization exercises be sure to reward the cat with treats and praise.

Do not overdo the desensitization; after all, loud sounds are supposed to be alarming to a cat. Just attempt to get your pet used to the level of noise that she would normally hear each day. Avoid setting the stereo or television too loud, and don't run around the house screaming and yelling!

FINICKY EATING

DESCRIPTION

Some cats seem to barely pick at their food throughout the day, perhaps eating a few bits here and there but never really appearing to chow down. Unlike dogs, who seem to gobble up everything in sight, most cats eat more selectively and slowly. This causes the owners of finicky cats to have to leave food down for the entire day, in order to satisfy these discriminating felines.

WHY YOUR CAT IS DOING THIS

Unlike dogs, cats seem to prefer eating small portions of food on a more frequent basis. This may cause your cat to appear to be a finicky eater. Look closer, though, and you will see that the food does disappear, albeit at a slower pace.

Some cats become spoiled by owners who feed them tasty little tidbits of human food throughout the day. When then presented with a boring dish of dry kibble, most pampered cats will look up as if to say, *"You're joking, right?"* The end result is a cat who will only eat human leftovers or food with lots of scent to it.

The biggest cause of finicky eating in a cat is the process of *free-feeding*. Most owners use this method of feeding, which involves leaving cat food out all day and replenishing it as the cat nibbles away at it, bit by bit. This procedure encourages your cat to eat very small amounts of food on an almost continuous basis throughout the day, giving him the appearance of being finicky. The food is always there; why should he become excited at dinnertime?

If your cat becomes sick or is injured, his appetite will fall off tremendously. If you notice that your cat's normally good appetite has taken a nosedive, it may point to a health problem.

SOLUTION

The best way to feed your cat is to establish defined feeding times during the day and make food available to him for a short window of time, say fifteen minutes or so. Twice a day put the cat's dish down with whatever food you decide to feed him while simultaneously ringing a bell or calling his name. Leave it down for fifteen minutes; if he eats, so be it. If not, pick the food up and store it. Later on in the day, repeat the procedure. If he eats, he eats. If not, remove the food. Eventually he will become hungry enough to get the picture. You may need to repeat this for a day or two; if so, don't worry. Your cat won't let himself starve. Sooner or later he will learn that when the dinner bell rings it's time to get that chow!

Avoid feeding your cat rich foods, as this will spoil him and turn him off his regular food. Limit treats as well, especially with a finicky or obese cat.

If your cat normally eats well but has just recently begun shunning food, take him to your veterinarian for a checkup. As stated, sudden changes in appetite can point to illness or injury, so be aware and get him to a professional as soon as you can. You might end up saving his life.

FLATULENCE

DESCRIPTION

No difficulty in describing this uncommon behavior. More of an inconvenience than a misbehavior, flatulence in cats occurs infrequently. When it does, however, it can be unpleasant and bothersome to owners, who are both embarrassed and inconvenienced by it.

WHY YOUR CAT IS DOING THIS

Often cats will become flatulent when a certain type of food is fed to them, often one that isn't one of the cat's staples, such as table scraps or milk products. Foods with too high a percentage of grains and not enough meat can also precipitate the problem. Cheap cat foods, high in fillers and fiber and low in meat, can often produce excess gas in a cat's intestines, due to high levels of bacterial fermentation, a process that takes place when lots of carbohydrates are present in the food.

Cats who are suffering from some type of intestinal disorder or are allergic to certain types of foods can become flatulent as well. Often this is accompanied by diarrhea, dehydration, and a reduced appetite.

SOLUTION

The first step in minimizing flatulence in your cat is taking him to the veterinarian to eliminate the possibility of intestinal disorders or allergic reactions to a certain type of food. He or she will also recommend a food for your cat, one that will help reduce the formation of gas in the intestinal tract.

Be sure to feed your cat a food that has meat as the first ingredient and not grains or filler material. Also, eliminate all table scraps from your cat's diet, as these can often accentuate the problem. Try not to change your cat's brand of food if he seems to be doing fine with it. Unnecessary changes in diet can lead to flatulence, as well as diarrhea, so stick with what works.

GARBAGE OR CUPBOARD RAIDING

DESCRIPTION

Some cats are smart enough to learn how to open a cupboard door to get at the tasty food or garbage hidden inside. A flick of the paw or a nudge with a nose is often all it takes for a determined feline to gain access to the "mother lode." The owner of such a curious cat comes home from work and finds refuse all over the kitchen floor or else discovers opened food packages from a pantry closet strewn all over the home, the satisfied kitty happily cleaning him- or herself off in a corner.

WHY YOUR CAT IS DOING THIS

Your cat is a smart, curious creature with a great sense of smell. If you are gone from the home and the cat is hungry, he will search for something to eat. If his food dish is empty, odds are he will go scouting around the home for something to satisfy his cravings. After checking the countertops, he will soon resort to scenting out something hidden behind a cupboard door. As many people keep their garbage pail in a cupboard under the kitchen sink, that's where their curious cats head first. Many cats will figure out how to flick the door open within a few minutes; if the garbage pail has an easily removed lid (or none at all), your pet has hit the jackpot.

Though much more common in dogs, cupboard raiding occurs in cats as well, particularly smart ones with big appetites. Even cats who have food readily available to them will often prefer to eat what they can find in cupboards, as the food found there tends to be more aromatic. Given a choice, your cat would probably choose a dish of human leavings over one of dry kibble any day.

SOLUTION

The solution to this problem is a fairly simple one. First, go out to the hardware store and purchase enough baby cupboard locks to cat-proof all the cupboards in question. Designed to prevent full access to a cupboard or drawer unless a short plastic catch is pushed in and released, these locks will prevent your cat from opening any cupboard or drawer with food or garbage in it. Installation usually requires a small portable drill and a screwdriver. Once these locks are in place, your cat won't stand a chance of getting into the contents of the cupboard and making a mess and possibly ingesting something toxic.

In addition to installing the baby cupboard locks, you should make an attempt to limit the amount of garbage you keep in the garbage pail. Fragrant items such as leftover tuna sandwiches or uneaten bacon should be taken straight out to the garbage can outside the home, so as not to drive the cat crazy with desire. Do the same with the pantry; try not to store food that has a strong aroma or that is in an open box or container there.

Last, make sure your cat is being fed the proper amount of food each day. Whether you free-feed him or feed him on a schedule, a cat who is not getting enough food each day will ultimately go looking for more.

GROOMING, AVERSION TO

DESCRIPTION

Some cats develop a dislike for being groomed and will either run away from or attempt to scratch or bite the person attempting to do so. Your cat may see the comb or brush and head for the hills or else assume a defensive posture, with her ears folded back, her tail lashing, and her body raised up and arched. She may even hiss and snarl or physically injure the groomer.

WHY YOUR CAT IS DOING THIS

Several reasons might explain why your cat might not enjoy being groomed. He might have had a bad experience at one time, with the person grooming him accidentally catching the comb or brush in a matted section of his coat, resulting in a painful pull on the skin. Or the cat might have had a groomer try to manhandle him at some point, physically restraining him in order to complete the procedure. As cats rarely forget an upsetting incident (and often hold grudges), just one upsetting grooming event can sour him on the procedure forever.

Other cats simply do not like to be handled for very long or object to having someone else do the job of grooming for them. Cats who left their respective litters at too young an age (before the eighth week) tend not to tolerate extended handling that well, as they never received the proper amount of socialization from their littermates and mother. The lack of physical interaction during those crucial weeks can spoil cats to intimate touch for the rest of their lives.

SOLUTION

Much of the solution to this problem focuses on prevention, as most cats who have developed a dislike for being groomed can rarely be convinced otherwise. The first step is making sure to adopt or purchase a kitten who has been allowed to stay with his or her mother and littermates until the eighth week. Doing so will help the kitten learn proper etiquette and socialization skills and allow him or her to participate in mutual grooming sessions with the whole feline family. A kitten from a well-rounded social situation will accept grooming from you much more readily than a kitten removed from his or her mother and littermates at too early an age.

Longhaired cats tend to dislike grooming more than their shorthaired kin, because of the greater chance of tangles or matted hair occurring. It also takes longer to groom longhaired cats, requiring them to tolerate the procedure for a greater period of time. Choosing a shorthaired breed will therefore help you avoid the problem, as they take only a few moments to brush out.

Whether you choose a longhaired or shorthaired cat, make sure to begin grooming sessions from the very start of your relationship. Handle your kitten as much as possible, rewarding him with occasional small treats during the procedure. Begin lightly running a comb through his fur once or twice each day, for a minute or so, again giving him treats during the session. Do the same with a brush. Be sure never to pull too hard, especially if you come across a mat or tangle. Gently work the mat or tangle out with the comb while keeping all tension off the skin. Make the process an enjoyable one, and your kitten will become a cooperative adult cat.

Limit grooming sessions to only a few minutes at a time to prevent your cat from growing bored or stressed. After a few minutes, quit, then reward your cat with a treat or a play session. Always be upbeat during grooming. Praise and reward him; make grooming seem like a fun game.

If your cat is showing a new dislike for grooming, he might have a sore spot or abscess on his skin.

Check for it; if you find something out of the ordinary, see your veterinarian.

Grooming an adult cat can often be more difficult than grooming a kitten. An adult cat with no grooming experience may object to being handled in such an intimate manner. Some, however, won't object at all and will actually enjoy the experience. It all depends on the individual cat. If your adult cat enjoys being petted and stroked, chances are he will take to being brushed and combed without much bother. Try the following procedure to groom an adult cat:

◆ Just before your cat's dinnertime, lure him over to you with a small treat. As you give him the treat with your right hand, stroke his back lightly with your left, from head to rump, all the time praising him softly.

◆ Continue giving him small treats with your right hand while stroking with your left. Then pick up a brush with your left hand and continue the stroking with it. Take care not to apply too much pressure at first. Just get him used to the feeling.

◆ After a minute of light brushing, end the session and feed him his dinner.

◆ Repeat this procedure once a day, gradually increasing the length and thoroughness of the brushing. Also, begin alternating the brush with a comb. Be gentle and upbeat and never force your will upon the cat.

If your adult cat simply hates to be groomed but must have it done, consider letting a professional groomer do the job. He or she has plenty of experience in dealing with stressed and unruly cats and will have the proper equipment and attitude to get the job done. If you do it, odds are your cat will become upset, and possibly he will hold a grudge against you. By allowing a groomer to "take the heat" you avoid damaging your relationship with the cat.

HANDLING, AVERSION TO

DESCRIPTION

Cats who dislike being handled tend to be a bit timid by nature and will conveniently disappear whenever guests arrive at the home. Rescued strays and shelter cats often tend to avoid prolonged handling, even from their owners. Your cat who dislikes being handled will often tolerate it for a short period, then either wander off or let the handler know of her displeasure by vocalizing or even scratching or biting. Even your relatively friendly cat can sometimes suddenly decide that she has had enough intimate contact and put a handling session to an end by walking away or by giving the handler a soft bite, as if to say, *"I have reached my limits."*

WHY YOUR CAT IS DOING THIS

Any one of several factors could explain why a cat has a low tolerance to handling. If your pet has experienced any form of physical abuse in the past, odds are she won't feel very comfortable being handled, even by a caring, gentle owner. A cat who has been teased and chased by children may have similar feelings. Rescued cats and longtime strays tend to become aloof and uncomfortable when being handled, as they have had to struggle to survive and may feel confined or endangered when required to stay in one place for an extended period of time, under the complete control of another. These cats shy away from handling because they need to feel in control and safe.

Your naturally timid or shy cat will usually allow you to handle her but may not be comfortable with guests trying to do the same. Again, the cat simply reaches a point where she feels pressured, unsafe, or out of control and must then put an end to the handling, even if it feels good.

Some well-adjusted cats (particularly unneutered ones) will abruptly decide that they have had enough handling, even though they might have been enjoying the attention right up to the moment of rejection. These cats seem to genuinely enjoy being touched but quickly reach a saturation point, whereupon they must break off the contact. They reach a point at which the discomfort of the situation overtakes the pleasure of being handling, causing them end the session.

Cats separated from their litter before the eighth week may not have received the proper amount of socialization needed to become well-rounded, confident adults. These cats often shun the physical attentions of others (particularly other cats). Though normally affectionate with their owners, this type of cat might object to being touched by guests.

SOLUTION

Certain steps can be taken to minimize this problem. First, never seek out and force your timid cat to accept handling. Instead, let the cat determine when and where she will accept touch from you. By allowing her this privilege you ensure that she actually wants to interact with you. When she does seem open to being handled, do so gently, taking care not to touch areas that she seems to object to, such as the rump or the neck area. End the handling session while she still seems to be enjoying it, to assure that the entire experience was enjoyable to her. Consider rewarding her with an occasional tasty treat during the handling session to reinforce and encourage the behavior.

Do not expect your hand-shy cat to accept handling from guests, particularly young children, who can be unpredictable and excessively rough at times. Do allow your guests to offer the cat treats, however; have them place the treat on the floor near their feet, encouraging the cat to come close. Eventually she should allow some minor handling to happen, even if it is limited to her brushing up against the person's legs.

To help prevent your cat from becoming hand-shy, make sure to handle her regularly from the first day you bring her home. Always be gentle, and always reward a good handling session with a treat or two. Make daily handling and grooming a part of the routine. Try to involve guests as well; let them handle the kitten whenever in the home, provided she is willing. Teach children to be gentle and to never force the kitten into being handled.

Consider not allowing your cat outdoors too often, as doing so can contribute greatly to a cat's apprehensions toward touch. When purchasing or adopting kittens or cats, be sure they enjoy being handled and stroked before taking them home. Watch their behavior with other cats and humans; if you see any antisocial behavior, choose another cat.

Never physically punish your cat, as this will probably cool her to handling. Cats remember unpleasant experiences and often hold grudges against an abuser for a very long time; hit your cat and you may lose her trust forever.

Consider having your cat neutered, as doing so will even out her temperament and remove the undesirable effects that hormonal peaks and valleys can have on mood and accessibility. Many cats become stressed and uneasy during a time of sexual arousal; this stress can cause them to act irrationally, particularly toward physical touch. An unneutered female with mating experience will be especially sensitive to touch during this time, as the entire mating procedure tends to be a painful one for her. Any form of physical contact while she is in heat could remind her of the mating act itself, in which the male restrains her by the neck, then inflicts great pain upon completing coitus.

HIDING

DESCRIPTION

Timid or fearful cats often disappear under sofas, tables, chairs, beds, or desks whenever anything unexpected happens. The arrival of guests will usually precipitate the behavior. Some cats if they feel the least bit unsure or fearful will even hide from their own owners. Hidden cats will normally not reappear until well after the perceived "threat" has left their territory. If made to face strangers, such cats could become defensive; they might hiss, scratch, or bite in order to regain their hiding place.

WHY YOUR CAT IS DOING THIS

Some cats are just plain shy. Whether this is caused by heredity or environmental experience, reserved, cautious cats easily becomes overwhelmed by new persons or situations presented to them. Though shyness is usually seen as a behavioral problem, don't forget that felines have for millions of years needed to be cautious, careful creatures in order to survive and succeed in the wild. Instinctively fearful of the unknown, cats in the wild have the uncanny ability to disappear silently into the forest or jungle and keep perfectly quiet and still until the perceived danger has passed. An effective survival tool, this instinct perseveres in the domestic cat and often shows up whenever the cat feels threatened.

That said, some domestic cat breeds are by nature much more cautious than others. Persians, for example, tend to be much more careful and timid than Siamese or Burmese and are much more likely to hide when strangers approach. Stray cats and those pets allowed to live most of their lives outdoors are much more likely to hide from strangers in the home, a result of having to hide from predators and other dangers outside.

Removing your cat from her familiar territory to a new, unfamiliar one can often cause her to hide on a regular basis. Being removed from the comfort and security of familiar surroundings and thrust into a strange and foreign place can overwhelm some cats, who initially assume that the new place already has established cats living in and around it, who claim the place for themselves. Being forced to invade another cat's domain can be very stressful to your cat, causing her to hide whenever anything unusual occurs.

SOLUTION

The cat who decides to hide whenever strangers show up obviously feels threatened and probably has a strong hereditary component driving the behavior. Because of this, it can often be difficult to modify. You can try, however, by first attempting to desensitize your cat to unpredictable events. Start by leaving a television or radio on while you are gone. Tune in to a station with lots of conversation happening, so the cat can slowly become used to the sound of persons talking.

Next, try to limit the number of places your cat can hide when guests come over. Place objects under the sofa and chairs, so that she has no place to hide, and close doors so that she can't run off and hide under a bed or in a closet.

When guests do come over, let them know what you are trying to do and inform them not to seek out the cat but simply sit calmly in one place. Progress can be something as small as having your cat in the same room as guests without her cowering or hissing.

Try putting your timid cat on a regular feeding schedule, instead of free-feeding her throughout the day. This will create times during the day at which she will feel truly hungry. By doing so you will be able to get her to respond to treat offerings more readily, especially right at or before mealtime. In addition, consider ringing a bell whenever you feed her, to condition her to believe that the sound means good things are about to happen. Then, invite a guest over at the cat's dinnertime. Have the guest prepare the food, place it down, ring the bell, then leave the kitchen. If the cat is hungry enough, she will come out of hiding to eat. In this way, you use one strong instinct, the food drive, to supersede another, namely, the fear of strangers. If this is done often enough, the cat will eventually come to see the appearance of a guest as a sign that delicious food is on the way.

HOUSE-SOILING PROBLEMS

DESCRIPTION

House soiling is always a major concern for cat owners, as any feline who fails to use his or her litter box makes life miserable for everyone in the home. The cat in question may choose to defecate or urinate in inappropriate spots, possibly ruining carpets, bedding, or flooring. Once a location has been chosen, the cat will often reuse it, further aggravating the owner. As cats normally prefer to cover their waste materials, the undesirable spot they choose to eliminate in is often a closet, bed, or dirty clothes pile, which provides the errant animal with materials to bury the "mistake" in. Sometimes the cat, if displaying marking behavior (an expression of territoriality), will urinate or "mark" extremely visible areas, such as beds, bedposts, and doorways.

WHY YOUR CAT IS DOING THIS

Many possible causes for improper cat elimination exist. They include the following.

Illness

Don't assume your cat is having accidents all over the home because he wants to make your life miserable. The chance exists that a medical condition is at fault. A kidney, bladder, stomach, or intestinal problem could cause your cat to lose control, as could an allergic reaction or even a poisoning episode. Cats who seem to have accidents in different spots each time, or are getting on in years have a greater chance of the problem being caused by a medical condition. Accidental defecation usually involves very runny stool, a clear sign of illness.

Litter Box Troubles

Your cat's litter box occupies a crucial place in his life. Proper disposing of feces and urine is an age-old feline drive, spurred on by cats' need to hide their identity and location from predators. In your home, your cat's preferred spot to eliminate is his litter box, where he will happily and carefully bury all waste materials.

Trouble can arise when the condition or location of the box changes. When this happens, the cat in question will seek out a new, clean place to eliminate, often unacceptable to the owner. Even changing brands of cat litter can upset your cat and cause him to abandon the litter box.

Obtaining a second cat but failing to purchase a second litter box can often prompt the less dominant animal to search out a more secure spot at which to eliminate. Unfortunately, that might end up being the floor of your closet.

Big Changes

As discussed earlier in the book, cats love a stable, predictable environment. Stirring the pot up in any way could provoke some cats into temporarily eschewing the litter box. Moving to a new home, acquiring a new pet, going on an extended vacation (while leaving kitty at home), or even rearranging furniture can do it, as can the loss or addition of a family member. The loss of an established pet companion can also cause your cat to become temporarily confused and depressed, possibly resulting in elimination mishaps.

Stress

Any stressful situation your cat experiences can affect his elimination habits. Abuse of any kind, territorial intrusion, illness, injury, or a change in environment can cause stress, resulting in accidents. Even a stray cat wandering around outside your home can stress your cat out enough to cause the problem. An unexpected bath or grooming session, dramatic weather change, or even a change in food can trigger improper elimination habits.

Marking Behavior

Cats are very territorial creatures. In the wild, they mark out the boundaries of their respective territories by urinating, defecating, scratching, and depositing scent from numerous glands in their bodies. Any competitive cat coming close to these marked-out boundaries gets the clear signal that he or she is not wanted. Other cats do the same with their own territories, allowing all the cats in the area to avoid unnecessary conflict. By respecting each other's domains, they also ensure that there will be enough prey to go around.

Cats do not normally spray urine or defecate inside their own territories unless a perceived threat to their status is sensed. A very dominant cat will certainly do so, particularly if a new pet or person has suddenly appeared in the home. Unneutered cats, particularly males, are much more likely to spray or defecate in the home, a way of marking territory or objecting to the presence of a perceived competitor. Furniture and doorways are likely spots to receive this very undesirable action.

Rescued strays and shelter cats, particularly those not yet neutered, are very apt to spray or defecate in the home, as they have had to do so while living outdoors. Often even neutering these cats won't have an immediate effect on the behavior, as it has become such an ingrained and reinforced habit.

Fecal marking is much rarer than spraying, but it can occur, especially among extremely dominant cats forced to suddenly cohabit a home with a new pet or pets. Indoor/outdoor cats living in a neighborhood with a high density of outdoor felines can often practice this behavior as well. The severely restricted territories each cat has often require them to take these drastic measures to mark out a small but valued domain. Any cat who resists instinct and instead chooses to leave feces unburied is clearly a dominant animal and extremely motivated to make a territorial statement.

SOLUTION

The first step in trying to solve a feline house-soiling problem is taking the cat to the veterinarian for a full examination to rule out any chance of illness causing the mishaps. Something as simple as a poorly tolerated new food could be responsible for the undesirable behavior. An infectious disease or some form of internal disorder might also be at fault. Trust your veterinarian to discover if any medical cause is at work; if so, he or she may be able to halt the problem quickly, with the right medication or the proper change in diet.

If you suspect the litter box is the cause of the house soiling, first make sure to scoop it out at least three times each day and change the litter completely at least twice a month. Be sure to locate the box in a quiet, low-traffic area, and try not to change the brand of litter you use, once your cat seems to approve of it. If you suspect a change in litter has precipitated the problem, try going back to the old brand. Doing so could end the problem overnight. If you have more than one cat, try adding a second litter box to the home, preferably in a different area. Doing so will ensure that your subordinate cat doesn't become intimidated by the presence of the more dominant feline in or near the only litter box in the home. He will instead have a "fallback" box to use, instead of a pile of clothes in your bedroom.

Try to avoid changing the box itself unless absolutely necessary. Cats get attached to the look and scent of the old one and might object to a newer design. If you must get a new one, leave the old one down for a while and place the new one next to it, filled with litter. In this way, your cat will have the comfort of the old box but be able to explore the new one in his own time.

Whenever possible, avoid major change in the cat's life. If you must move to a new home, consider confining your cat to one room for a few days until you are sure he is not having any accidents. Then allow him access to the rest of the home, being careful to observe him closely for a few days. Also, if moving into a new rental home be sure to first clean any carpets there with an effective-odor-neutralizing product, available at all good pet stores. This will eliminate the odor of pets who lived there previously, preventing your cat from spraying as a means of claiming territory.

Avoid remodeling unless necessary. Changing the look of your home alters your cat's territorial layout, making it seem a bit alien. If your cat feels uncomfortable, he could develop a house-soiling problem. If change has to occur, try doing so gradually, perhaps one room at a time. Also, avoid buying used furniture, which often has the scent of other animals on it.

It goes without saying that stress can cause all manner of behavior problems, including house soiling.

Try, then, to keep things on an even keel; don't allow toddlers to chase and pull on your cat, and don't introduce other pets into the home unless necessary. Keeping your cat safe and secure will go a long way in preventing all types of behavior problems, including house soiling.

Taking a cat into your home and asking him to completely ignore the drive to mark his territory is a difficult task (from an evolutionary standpoint) but necessary if you both are to get along. Domestication requires cats to change many natural behaviors in order to fit into their new homes. Your cat simply cannot be allowed to spray or defecate in your home.

The first and most important step you can take to prevent marking in the home is having your cat neutered. An unneutered cat will spray in the home, especially when sensing the presence of strangers or other animals in and around the home. Both males and females can be guilty of this behavior; removing the effects of the mating drive will make your cat much more pleasant to live with and much less likely to feel the need to mark.

If your cat has sprayed or defecated in the home, you must clean the area thoroughly in order to prevent a repeat performance in the same spot. Use an odor neutralizer product (available in all pet stores). If you see your cat nosing around and getting ready to mark, spray him with water from a plant sprayer while simultaneously saying, *"No!"* If he seems to be targeting just one area, treat the spot with a commercially available cat repellant or try sprinkling black pepper on the area. Also try placing strips of double-sided tape down around the area, as cats hate the sticky feeling on the bottoms of their feet. Strips of aluminum foil can also work, as can shallow pans of water or crinkled sheets of newspaper. If all else fails, try placing small dishes of food down at the spot. Cats never mark near food, so this might help break the habit.

If nothing has worked to eliminate the marking behavior, try confining your cat to a small room or wire cage for a week or two. Minimizing his territory in such a way gives the cat little reason to mark. After a week or two, try slowly introducing him back into the rest of the home, making sure that all old marked areas have been cleaned with an odor-neutralizing product.

HYGIENE PROBLEMS

DESCRIPTION

A big reason we love cats is their meticulous cleaning habits. Partly as a result of instinct and partly as a result of learning from mother and siblings early on, most felines keep themselves quite clean, spending much of the day primping, licking, and tidying themselves.

The rare cats who fail to keep themselves clean will begin to retain dirt and various skin secretions on their coat, eventually causing them to take on a bad odor (much like a dog, who depends on us for bathing). Longhaired cats tend to suffer from this more than the shorthaired varieties, due to the additional length of coat. The outdoor cat is far more likely to have bad hygiene habits than one kept indoors exclusively. The cat with bad hygiene is also more likely to act sullenly or in an antisocial manner.

WHY YOUR CAT IS DOING THIS

Most cats who exhibit poor hygiene habits tend to have a medical problem of some type brewing. Cleaning is such a routine behavior for a cat that the absence of it can easily mean injury or illness of some kind, perhaps minor, perhaps serious. Infectious disease, hidden injury, internal disorder, parasitic infestation, abscess, toxic poisoning, or even urinary tract disease can cause cats to disregard their personal hygiene habits.

Sometimes obese cats (particularly a longhaired one) will fail to properly clean themselves, due to their inability to reach all of the necessary spots on their bodies, particularly around the anal area. Cats with badly matted hair will often not be able to properly clean all the dirt from their-coat, as the mats tend to act as dirt magnets.

Outdoor cats will often become quite dirty in comparison to indoor cats. If the dirt is of the oily kind, the cat won't be able to remove it and might actually become sick trying to do so.

SOLUTION

If your cat's personal hygiene habits have suddenly taken a turn for the worse, take her to your veterinarian as soon as possible, as she could be ill or injured. He or she will make that determination; if something is detected, odds are it will be easily dealt with by the doctor. The hygiene problem should clear up along with the medical problem. Once your cat feels better, she will get right back to cleaning herself up nicely.

If your dirty cat is also obese, you will need to put her on a diet and get her moving around a bit more to burn some calories. While doing so be sure to bathe the cat at least once a month. If she tends to put up a fight at the thought of being bathed, let your local groomer take on the task. Once your cat is clean, you will need to keep her brushed out, particularly if she is a longhaired breed, like a Persian or Maine coon cat. Once she is able to again reach all of her body parts, she should once again take care of the problem herself.

If your cat is becoming excessively dirty outdoors, consider keeping her in the home or at least reducing the time she spends out there. If she gets any type of oil on her coat, you must remove it through bathing. Take her to a groomer if necessary, but get the toxic substances off her coat. Also, try to locate the source of the mess, then clean it up, to prevent future problems. As the outdoor cat tends to get dirtier than the indoor variety, consider grooming your outdoor cat more often, to deal with the mess and to help her cut down on her own grooming time. Cats who spend too much time cleaning themselves are more prone to hairballs, so try keeping them as clean as possible.

INCESSANT LICKING, SCRATCHING, OR BITING

DESCRIPTION

Cats are famous for cleaning themselves on a regular basis. Sometimes the behavior can become incessant, however, and can include scratching as well. Such cats will appear to never be quite happy with their state of hygiene and will lick and scratch themselves constantly, often until their fur falls out and their skin becomes red and raw. These cats will become miserable and will often refuse to interact with their owners or anyone else. Often the animal's appetite will suffer, causing a loss of weight.

WHY YOUR CAT IS DOING THIS

The usual cause of this behavior is a parasitic infestation, generally either fleas, mites, or lice. Though fastidious about keeping clean, your cat won't be able to fully rid himself of these pesky little creatures, which, if left unchecked, will continue to multiply, making the problem worse. Cats allowed access to the outdoors suffer the most from this problem.

An ongoing disorder of the skin, commonly referred to as *dermatitis*, can also cause incessant licking and scratching. Dermatitis can cause rashes, itchiness, dandruff, and, in severe cases, serious infection. Three basic types of dermatitis exist: *allergic, contact*, and *parasitic*. All three can bring on the behavior. *Allergic dermatitis* is normally brought on by cats having an allergic reaction to a food they have eaten. The skin becomes red and itchy, causing such cats to lick, scratch, and bite themselves. *Contact dermatitis* is normally brought on when the cat's skin comes into contact with an irritating substance, such as a solvent, insecticide, shampoo, or cleaner. The symptoms are similar to those of allergic dermatitis but can often occur in very specific regions of the body. An example would be a cat who develops an intolerance to a type of flea collar; the skin around his or her neck becomes red and itchy, while the rest of the body remains normal. Outdoor cats tend to suffer from contact dermatitis more often than do indoor cats, as they have access to all manner of potentially harmful chemicals. *Parasitic dermatitis* is caused by the reaction your cat's skin has to the parasite in question; in addition to the irritation of the parasite's movements, the skin becomes red and inflamed from the actions of the parasite, causing further licking, scratching, and biting.

Some cats, particularly those allowed outdoors, become so dirty that they have no choice but to constantly lick and scratch in an attempt to get clean. If the dirt in question is of an oily nature, the cat won't have much luck removing it and could become quite ill after ingesting some of the material.

Stress is another potential cause for incessant licking and scratching. Subordinate cats in a multiple-cat home often become stressed at being picked on or dominated; one of the classic symptoms of this stress is constant grooming. Called *displacement behavior*, the grooming becomes a way of releasing tension or redirecting the stress of the moment. Humans and dogs practice displacement behavior, too, often yawning during times of stress or intimidation. It is a way for the mind to deny or ignore the upsetting situation. Sexual frustration can cause this as well; unneutered cats cut off from the outside will often incessantly groom themselves, to the point of absurdity.

Boredom can also cause your cat to overgroom himself. With not enough to do, he may begin passing the time by licking and scratching away. Chronic boredom can cause animals and humans alike to perform meaningless and redundant behaviors, such as overeating, foot or finger tapping, vocalizing, and pacing.

SOLUTION

The first step in solving the problem is to take your cat to your friendly veterinarian for a thorough checkup to determine if parasitic, contact, or allergic dermatitis is the cause of the incessant licking and scratching. Discovering parasites will be easy, as will getting rid of them. Diagnosing contact or allergic dermatitis can take longer, however; the veterinarian must rely on numerous tests, as well as lots of experience, to properly diagnose the situation. Once this is done, however, you can eliminate from your cat's life the food or substance causing the problem. When the problem has been diagnosed and treated, you should seriously consider keeping your cat indoors to prevent further infestation or contact with irritating substances. Indoor cats rarely suffer from dermatitis of any kind, except for food-based allergic reactions. Keep kitty inside, and parasites and irritants won't have a chance to do any damage.

If the cat in question is suffering from the stress of being picked on by other cats, try providing several food and water dishes and at least one extra litter box. Taking these steps should reduce the number of run-ins and allow the subordinate cat to eat and eliminate in peace. Be sure to allot ample play time for all the cats in the home and provide them with the largest indoor territory possible by opening doors to all the rooms in the home. Expanding the indoor territory in this way will lower territorial stresses and give the subordinate cat somewhere to go when being lorded over by the dominant animal.

To prevent this type of territorial stress, think hard before adding any more cats to an already established cat's domain. If you want to have two cats, obtain them both when they are kittens. Doing so will ensure that they get along well, with as little fighting as possible. Bringing a second kitten or adult cat into an established cat's home will often result in constant fireworks and stress for everyone. Avoiding that stress from the start will help prevent nervous behaviors like incessant licking and scratching.

Cats who lick and scratch out of boredom simply need more to occupy their time. Be sure to provide your cat with a rich environment. Do whatever you need to in order to relieve your cat's boredom. Doing so might just help stop the incessant licking and scratching and create a happier cat in the process.

JUMPING ONTO COUNTERS OR FURNITURE

DESCRIPTION

Cats have the enviable ability to leap onto surfaces many times higher than their height. Unfortunately, this allows them to jump onto counters and furniture at the least desirable times. Typically, this will happen in the kitchen while you are preparing food or at the dinner table while you and your family are trying to eat a meal. Or it may occur while you are sitting in a chair reading or watching television; many owners prefer that their cats not jump up onto them at these times but can't seem to control the behavior.

WHY YOUR CAT IS DOING THIS

Your cat will always be attracted to the scent of food. When you prepare a meal for yourself or your family, the cat will naturally smell the food and often jump up to investigate. Likewise, if you leave food out on the counters, sooner or later your cat will investigate the situation. The same goes for the dinner table; if not taught otherwise, your cat will probably jump up there whenever food is present, especially if you are in the habit of sometimes offering little tidbits to the cat from your plate.

Most well-adjusted cats will want to jump up into your lap while you are sitting in a chair or on the sofa, because they enjoy your company and want to be petted and stroked by you. The behavior becomes automatically reinforced each time you reward the cat with a pat on the head. Sometimes a few family members or guests dislike the behavior, while others enjoy it. The few who like having the cat on them will reinforce the behavior, much to the dismay of those who dislike it.

SOLUTION

With regard to keeping your cat off the kitchen counters, the first step is to make sure no food items are ever left out to entice the cat. Even items in a wrapper, cookie jar, or box should be removed and stored in a cupboard or refrigerator. Also, be sure to leave countertops clean and free of food remnants, including crumbs. Wiping them down with a soapy sponge afterward will further discourage your cat, as the soap will leave behind a bitter taste.

Next, never reward any begging behavior. Doing so will encourage your cat to appear whenever you are close to or working with food. Also, avoid giving your cat table scraps, as this will encourage her to like human foods (usually available when you are preparing or eating a meal).

Put your cat on a regular feeding schedule so you can better predict when she will be hungry. Then, feed her right before you begin preparing your own dinner, so she won't be hungry when human food is brought out. Also, never feed her scraps from your plate during dinner.

Keep a spray bottle filled with water with you during food preparation as well as at the dinner table. If your cat jumps up onto the counter or table, immediately spray her while saying, *"No!"* Even if no food is out on the counter or table, spray her and say, *"No!"* in order to get the message across that she isn't allowed up there. To prevent her from jumping up onto counters while you are away, place double-sided tape onto the countertops. If that fails to work, take a piece of chicken wire big enough to cover much of the counter and then place it atop the counter, making sure to raise it up about an inch from the counter surface. You can use a few strategically placed books to do this. Your cat will not be able to find decent footing with the chicken wire placed in such a manner and will give up quickly.

Preventing your cat from jumping up onto furniture can be a bit more difficult, as the furniture is a part of her environment. If you simply do not want her on any piece of furniture, you will need to keep a few spray bottles handy. The moment she jumps up onto a chair, for instance, spray her and say, *"No!,"* even if no one is currently in the chair. To stop her from going on the furniture while you are gone, try placing a few strips of double-sided tape on the seat of the chair (or cushions of the sofa). The sticky feeling on her paws will quickly dissuade her from repeating the act. Or try leaving a sheet of aluminum foil atop the sitting surface, for the same reason.

Whatever behavior modification technique you use, continue doing so for at least three or four weeks, in order to permanently modify the behavior. The idea is to get the thought out of your cat's mind permanently; to do so, you need to keep up the modification technique for a while. Eventually she should get the idea. Just remember to always have a spray bottle handy, keep food off the counters, and never encourage begging.

KNEADING

DESCRIPTION

Some cats develop the peculiar (to us) habit of kneading their paws on people in a repetitive, rhythmic fashion. Often accompanied by soft, happy purring, this behavior normally occurs when your cat is happy and relaxed, often while lying on or beside you. Though this behavior is endearing, some cats extend their claws while kneading, resulting in pain to the recipient.

WHY YOUR CAT IS DOING THIS

A common behavior of nursing kittens, the kneading action is thought to help encourage the mother cat's mammary glands to produce more milk. To the kitten, the action becomes associated with contentment and security. Many cats carry this behavior over into adulthood and apply it to their owners, often seen as surrogate mothers.

SOLUTION

Kneading only becomes an unpleasant behavior when the cat in question has exceedingly sharp claws that become extended during the process. If your cat does not extend his claws, the behavior remains endearing and needs no correction. If he does extend his claws, consider wearing protective clothing. As you can probably predict when the kneading sessions will occur (usually at bedtime or in the morning), wearing long pants and a long-sleeved shirt at those times will prevent any pain to you. Next, make sure that your cat's claws are trimmed at least five or six times a year, either by you or by a professional groomer. Doing so will prevent them from getting long enough to seriously scratch you.

If you decide to trim your cat's nails, you will need to start when he is a kitten, as most adult cats won't take too kindly to the procedure. Purchase a good-quality cat nail clipper from your pet shop, then place the kitten in your lap. Gently press on a foot pad to extend the claws of one foot, then carefully trim off no more than one-sixteenth of an inch. Be sure not to cut into the visible vein that runs down the center of each nail, as this will cause bleeding and pain. Take your time with the kitten; if necessary, do only one foot at a time. If you have any misgivings about cutting his nails (or if you have an adult cat who has never had experienced the procedure), let a professional do it.

MARKING AND SPRAYING (SEE "HOUSE-SOILING PROBLEMS.")

OLD AGE, BEHAVIOR PROBLEMS RELATED TO

DESCRIPTION

Cats are living longer and longer these days. A twelve- or thirteen-year-old feline used to be ancient; now cats routinely live as long as eighteen to twenty years, due mostly to better medical care and healthier foods. Often a ten-year-old cat will appear no worse off than one half that age. Only in the final few years of life do cats begin to show distinct signs of the aging process. Your older cat might become more irritable, particularly toward other pets. She may not respond to your calls as quickly, due to progressive hearing loss. Cataracts may blur her vision somewhat, causing her to miss visual cues. Her reflexes will be slower, as will her strength. A jump that used to be kitten's play to her five years earlier now becomes impossible, due to stiffer joints and weaker muscles. She may vocalize more due to aches and pains and may want to spend more time indoors if she has access to the outside. Older cats will often seek out the warmest spot in the home and stay there. Your cat's coat might become dirtier, due to stiffer joints not allowing her to groom as she used to. She might have trouble getting into her litter box, especially if it is located up high (to avoid the family dog) or if it has a high lip on it. Your older cat may become heavier, due to a slowing metabolism. Her teeth may begin to fall out. Her coat may become less dense and may dry out and become brittle. Last, your older cat's house-training habits could take a turn for the worse, due to an aging digestive tract.

WHY YOUR CAT IS DOING THIS

Quite simply, she is, as are all of us, getting older. The aging process slowly but surely takes its toll on the feline metabolism and organ systems. Cells that once renewed themselves easily no longer do so. Senses dull, and joints may become stiff and painful from the onset of arthritis. Poor circulation causes her to seek out warmer areas of the home. A slowing metabolic rate causes her to gain weight, despite no increase in food intake. Flexibility is down, causing her to attempt less feline acrobatics. Mice who never stood a chance now routinely get away. Failing organ systems make her more susceptible to infectious diseases, as well as tumors. As her liver and kidneys decline, urinary tract problems can arise.

Obviously, none of this is your cat's fault. When we reach our seventies and eighties, we may be cranky and difficult and frail, too. Your aged cat who loses patience with a child or young cat is only expressing her frustration at not being able to deal with life the way she used to. House-training accidents rarely are caused by behavioral problems at an advanced age but are usually physiological in nature instead. You cannot modify the behavior but can only work around it by altering the cat's environment to suit the problem.

SOLUTION

Until someone discovers how to reverse the aging process, we won't have many successful methods available for correcting undesirable behavior in the aged cat. Several techniques can be implemented, however, to minimize age's effects on your cat's behavior and well-being. They include:

◆ Increasing visits to your veterinarian to monitor the aging process more closely and catch serious problems (such as diabetes or cancer) as soon as possible.

◆ Close monitoring of the cat's appetite and

weight in order to prevent obesity, tooth and gum problems, and problems with digestion. Possible dietary changes could be in store, to ensure proper nutrition.

◆ Increased grooming sessions, to help your cat keep clean.

◆ Locating the litter box in a more easily accessible spot. You may also need to lower the lip on the litter box, if it is higher than six inches.

◆ Avoiding the introduction of new pets into your aged cat's home, which might annoy her and perhaps cause her to stress or overexert herself.

◆ Bringing her into the home on a full-time basis, if she is an outdoor cat, to keep her warm and prevent injury and infection. The older cat's immune system is not nearly as efficient at fending off contagions; bringing her into the home and away from other cats who might be carrying disease is best.

◆ Starting a program of gentle massage to help loosen up stiff joints and muscles and to increase circulation.

◆ Regular gentle exercise to delay the aging process. A five-minute play session each day can be all it takes.

OVERACTIVE BEHAVIOR

DESCRIPTION

Overactives cat seem to be "on" all the time. They are constantly moving, investigating, pestering people, and getting into all manner of trouble. Owners of this type of cat often cannot get a moment's peace; these cats are seemingly always underfoot, almost as if someone has been secretly giving them coffee instead of water.

WHY YOUR CAT IS DOING THIS

Several factors can causes a cat to act in an overactive manner. First, the breed of the cat should be taken into consideration. Certain breeds tend to be on average much more active than others. Those known to be on the active side include:

- ◆ Abyssinian
- ◆ Balinese
- ◆ Burmese
- ◆ Cornish Rex
- ◆ Devon Rex
- ◆ Egyptian Mau
- ◆ Havana Brown
- ◆ Japanese Bobtail
- ◆ Korat

- ◆ Ocicat
- ◆ Oriental
- ◆ Siamese
- ◆ Snowshoe
- ◆ Somali
- ◆ Sphynx
- ◆ Tonkinese

If you have previously owned other breeds or possibly mixed-breed cats, having one of the aforementioned hot rods might come as a shock to you at first, as they are all naturally energetic and curious animals.

Another possible cause of overactive behavior could simply be that the cat has not yet matured fully. Kittens and adolescent cats always have a much higher activity level than do mature adults. Once your cat reaches ten to twelve months of age, however, he should begin to slow down a bit.

An unneutered cat will have a higher activity level than a neutered one, driven by hormones. Once your unneutered cat reaches sexual maturity, he will want to get out and find a mate. Barring him from doing so will result in restlessness, as well as a host of other undesirable behaviors, including destructive behavior, excessive vocalization, spraying, and possibly fecal marking.

Switching your outdoor cat over to indoor-only living can also result in restless overactivity, as he had been used to a much larger territory, with many more stimuli to keep him amused. Limited to the home, this pet will, at least for a time, appear to be stressed and overactive. The same is true for strays and rescued cats, who often come from outdoor situations.

Diet can play a role in the activity levels of some cats. For instance, certain commercial cat foods, particularly ones in the "semimoist" category, contain high amounts of sugar, which can be known to cause hyperactivity in animals and humans. Too much protein in the diet can have the same effect on a cat. Though felines do require high levels of protein, too much can raise metabolism and stress the kidneys.

Boredom and isolation can be a big cause of overactive behavior in cats. Leave your cat alone all day with little to amuse himself with and he might start bouncing off the walls for entertainment. When you do finally come home, he can't seem to leave you be; you become the target for all his frustrations. It appears to you or others that he is overactive when, in fact, he is just releasing all of his pent-up energy.

SOLUTION

If your hot rod cat is still under a year in age, give him a little more time to mature. He should begin to slow down enough to make the relationship more rewarding. Don't try using negative methods in order to slow your kitty down, as active, curious play is vital to his development.

If your overactive cat has not been neutered, now might be a good time to take care of that. All of that pent-up sexual energy has no place to go; by neutering him you relieve him of the stress and allow him and you to bond more closely. He will be calmer and happier. If you decide to have your adult cat neutered, hormonal effects will lasts for several months past the procedure, then gradually reduce to zero by the fifth or sixth month.

If your cat has just recently been switched over to an indoor-only existence, try to give him time to adapt to the smaller territory. Help him along by making the home a fun place to live; put lots of interesting cat toys down and get him a multitiered, carpeted "kitty condo" to call his own. Place a cardboard box filled with newspaper down on the floor. Hide a few treats around the place. Doing so will help him readjust more quickly. Though it may take as long as six months for him to calm down and accept the new arrangement, it is well worth doing, from a safety and health standpoint. The same goes for a bored, isolated cat; make the home more interesting.

Try not to feed your cat any food high in sugar, as this can result in overactivity and poor overall health. Also, check the protein content of your cat's food with your veterinarian to ensure that it isn't too high.

OVEREATING

DESCRIPTION

Though most cats don't seem to have an overactive appetite, some become so enamored of food that their increased weight begins to affect their health. Obese cats are much more common now than they were a few decades ago, due partially to fewer cats having access to the outdoors, as well as the feline becoming a much more desired pet, especially in urban environments. The more pampered your cat is, the better chance of his becoming spoiled and overweight.

WHY YOUR CAT IS DOING THIS

Simple answer: look in the mirror! That's right; your cat's eating habits are completely governed by you, her owner. She cannot open the refrigerator and pull out a snack any time she wants one. You have to provide her with food. Thus any weight gain she shows (except that due to a hormonal imbalance) is because of your actions.

Owners who free-feed (make food available for their cats all day) run the risk of teaching their pets to eat a little bit of food many times par day. As most owners tend to top off the dish whenever it looks low, cats who free-feed runs the risk of eating much more than they actually need. Over the course of a few years this can result in obesity.

Another big cause of overeating among cats is treat giving. Whether prompted by begging or meted out randomly, treats can add up over the course of a day and result in obesity. A spoiled cat who receives treats and table scraps throughout the day learns to expect them and becomes conditioned to the regular offerings. Consumption of such a cat's regular food rarely goes up, however, because it simply does not taste as good as the scrumptious tidbits coming from your plate or from the refrigerator.

Sometimes a dominant cat will steal food from a submissive feline housemate without the owner knowing. Through intimidation, your imposing cat will often eat her food as well as her poor submissive counterpart's before you can ever even notice. This often happens when a new kitten or cat is brought into an established cat's domain. The new cat loses weight while the dominant cat gains.

Infrequently a cat will suffer from an underactive thyroid gland. Called *hypothyroidism*, the condition slows down the cat's metabolism, causing his or her body to burn fewer calories, even though he or she still is eating the same amount of food as usual. Though the metabolism is slowed down, the appetite remains the same, causing weight gain.

SOLUTION

The first step is to take your cat in to your veterinarian for a checkup. He or she will first determine if the cat has a thyroid imbalance. If she does, the condition can be corrected through medication. Your veterinarian will also determine how overweight your cat is and what her target weight should be. Most veterinarians will also offer helpful feeding tips and can often suggest a different, lower-calorie food to feed your pet.

The next step in curtailing your cat's overeating is to switch to a regular feeding schedule, instead of free-feeding. By doing so you will be able to determine exactly how much food she is eating each day. Once that is known, you can then cut her food by 10 or 15 percent in an effort to get her back down to a reasonable weight. A regular feeding schedule will also stabilize her appetite; you will be better able to predict just when she will be hungry. By knowing that, you can feed her an exact amount at an exact time, instead of randomly filling and refilling a dish all day, never knowing exactly how much food the cat is really eating.

Your overweight cat should not be receiving treats and table scraps throughout the day, no matter how she begs or how much you enjoy giving them to her. Excess treats will add up and create an obese cat, who will in turn live an average of five years less than a cat at or near his or her ideal body weight. Do not encourage begging by giving treats, especially while you are at the dinner table. The only time to give treats is when you are teaching a new behavior to your cat and you need to reward her. That's it. Remember: if you love her, cut out the spoiling! If she has already learned to beg, teach her that the behavior is not appropriate by spraying her with your trusty plant sprayer bottle while saying, "*No!*" Eventually she will get the idea. Also, make sure that all family members refrain from feeding her extra tidbits. The behavior won't change unless all family members participate.

If one of your cats is gaining weight while the other is losing, odds are the chunky one is eating the thin one's food while you are not looking. To prevent this, try supervising them at dinnertime. Make sure to have separate dishes located on opposite sides of the kitchen. Watch them to see if theft is actually happening. If it is, simply begin feeding them in separate rooms.

Consider weighing your overweight cat at least once par week to chart her weight gain or loss. To do so, simply pick her up, weigh both of you, then weigh yourself. Subtract your weight from the combined weight to determine her own.

Once you have your cat at the weight your veterinarian prescribed, make a real effort to keep her there. Be exact with the amount you feed her. As little as an once or two too much at every meal can, over a year or two, add up to three, four, or five extra pounds. For an animal who is supposed to weigh under ten pounds, that's a huge increase.

PILL TAKING, AVERSION TO

DESCRIPTION

Cats can be difficult to administer pills to. Not nearly as compliant as dogs in this area, the resistant cat will often squirm, try to escape, scratch, or bite in an attempt to avoid the procedure. If your cat is successful in his attempt to escape, he will hide from you and may avoid physical contact with you for quite some time.

WHY YOUR CAT IS DOING THIS

Most cats are very concerned about their private space and consider having someone's fingers jammed down their throats invasion of their personal space, as would most of us. Yours will not want anyone (including you) to intrude past his comfort zone. Some level of resistance is therefore to be expected from your cat during this procedure, especially if you have never tried it before.

SOLUTION

There may be times when you must administer a medication to your cat in order to help him recover from an illness. It therefore becomes vital to be able to medicate the cat in some way. Fortunately, many medications are available in powder form, which can simply be sprinkled onto a spoon of canned cat food and given to the cat at mealtime. Any medication in capsule form can also be opened up and sprinkled onto food. Even solid pills can be crushed into a powder and mixed into food. If using this method, make sure that the cat is hungry to ensure that he will eat all of the canned food offered. (To do so, be sure to have your cat on a regular feeding schedule in order to better predict when he will be hungry. Cats who free-feed rarely have strong, predictable appetites; because of this, they may not want to eat the canned offering laced with the medicine.)

The best way to ensure that your cat will take a pill when needed is to train him from kittenhood to do so. First, make sure that you handle the kitten from the very first day, including grooming as well as a daily inspection of his body, paws, ears, and mouth. After each handling session, always give him a treat as a reward. After you have accustomed him to regular handling, you can begin to practice the pill-giving technique. Try it at first with a feline vitamin pill or with no pill at all, just to get the technique down. The technique is as follows:

1. Hold the pill between the thumb and index finger of one hand.
2. Place your other hand atop your kitten's head. Put the thumb and index finger of this hand into the corners of the kitten's mouth, hooking them in slightly, so that the fingertips are in past the molars.
3. Tilt the kitten's head back until his nose points straight up. His mouth should now open wide enough to accept a pill.
4. Quickly place the pill onto the back-center portion of the kitten's tongue.
5. Close his mouth, and hold it closed for a few seconds while gently massaging his throat. This will ensure that he swallows the pill.

With practice, you will get very fast at performing this technique. Don't try this with an adult cat who doesn't tolerate handling very well, however, as you could be bitten or scratched.

If all else fails, you can go to your pet store and purchase a "pill gun," which will quickly and painlessly shoot the pill back into the cat's throat. Always reward the cat afterward with a treat and praise.

PLANT EATING

DESCRIPTION

Many cat owners enjoy keeping houseplants in the home. Unfortunately, many cats develop a habit of munching on the plants, much to the dismay of the owners. Even those in the garden outside can often fall prey to the veggie-loving feline. Young plants are especially at risk. Unfortunately, this annoying behavior can also be potentially dangerous for your cat, as many house- and garden plants are quite toxic to felines. The list of toxic plants includes:

◆ Azalea
◆ Bean plants
◆ Cactus
◆ Crocus
◆ Daffodil
◆ Dieffenbachia
◆ Hemlock
◆ Hydrangea
◆ Ivy
◆ Lily

- Marijuana
- Mistletoe
- Mushrooms
- Narcissus
- Nightshade
- Oleander
- Philodendron
- Poinsettia
- Potato leaves
- Rhododendron
- Tobacco
- Tomato leaves
- Walnuts
- Yew

WHY YOUR CAT IS DOING THIS

Though cats are true carnivores, they do sometimes consume vegetable matter, especially in the wild, when cats consume their prey's stomach and its contents. Stomach contents of prey animals usually include partially digested vegetable matter, which, when eaten by cats, can provide them with vitamins and minerals not necessarily found elsewhere.

Domestic cats seem to love chewing on and eating plants; why is not completely clear. Several reasons could explain the behavior, however. The cats may be instinctively searching for nutrients not provided to them in their regular diets. Or some cats may feel the need to vomit up something disagreeable, like a big hairball or other undesirable object and eating enough plant material can have this effect on them. Another possible reason for the plant munching is simply that they like the taste and texture of what they are eating. Just look at many felines' obsession with catnip, a perennial in the mint family.

SOLUTION

Clearly this behavior should be minimized, not only for the sake of the pretty plant but for the safety of the cat as well. The first step to take is to avoid purchasing plants known to be toxic to cats. Houseplants such as the philodendron, dieffenbachia, and ivy, so common in many households, should be either avoided or hung from the ceiling in such a way as to completely prohibit access by the cat. If your cat has access to the outdoors, be sure to avoid planting the toxic shrubbery and garden plants listed previously.

Unfortunately, you won't be able to stop her from going over to the neighbor's yard, if she is an outdoor cat. You will have to decide if allowing her this privilege is important enough.

Locate whatever nontoxic houseplants you have off of the floor, either in tall stands or from hanging mounts. Plant pedestals should be high, and as narrow as the plant's draining dish, so as to give the cat no footing whatsoever. Never keep any plants on the floor or on shelves with easy cat access.

Cover the soil of the plant with marbles or rocks to discourage digging. Wipe down the plant leaves with a diluted soap-and-water mixture; it won't hurt the plant, and it will taste terrible to the cat. You can also purchase a veterinarian-approved cat repellant and apply it to the plant.

Also try placing double-sided tape around the area where you keep your plants in an effort to dissuade your cat from going near. Try aluminum foil strips as well. In severe cases, place mousetraps *underneath* multiple sheets of newspaper around the plants. When sprung, the traps will slap harmlessly into the paper, making a loud sound but not harming the cat. Be sure not to place the traps atop the newspaper, however, as your cat could be seriously hurt. If you can catch the cat in the act of chewing on a plant, spray her with water from a plant sprayer bottle.

While discouraging your cat from going near your prized houseplants you should simultaneously provide her with some grass seedlings to chew on as much as she likes. Grow them yourself from grass seed or purchase them at your local pet store. Place them far from your houseplants, perhaps in the kitchen, near where she eats. When given an alternative like this, most cats will forget about the houseplants entirely.

Last, try to keep your cat's environment as stimulating as possible to prevent boredom, one of the main causes of improper behavior. Lots of toys and other objects to investigate, as well as plenty of play time with you, should keep her nose out of your houseplants.

PUSHY OR RUDE BEHAVIOR

DESCRIPTION

Some cats like to get into the middle of everything. Try to sit down and read a book, and your cat immediately jumps into your lap and rubs all over you, seeking your attention. Or try to give a little attention to another pet in the family, and your pushy cat immediately gets in between you and the other animal, insisting that you pay attention only to him. Pushy, rude cats seem to think that the entire world revolves around them. They can't bear to be ignored and act in a dominant fashion toward all other members of the home (including humans). Such felines insist on greeting, eating, and investigating first and even using the litter box before other cats. In a nutshell, your pushy, rude cat thinks he is king of the castle.

WHY YOUR CAT IS DOING THIS

In a very real way, domestic cats, especially those kept exclusively indoors, remain in an adolescent frame of mind all their lives. By taking responsibility for your cat's food, shelter, security, and entertainment from kittenhood on, you prevent him from fully maturing psychologically. In a sense, your cat remains forever a teenager.

Nevertheless, he still maintains all of the instincts

inherent in a cat, including the desire to establish some level of control over his environment. Each cat possesses an inherent degree of dominance. Some simply think more of themselves than others and go about expressing that quality in their everyday lives. So, imagine, if you will, a particularly dominant cat, forever frozen within an adolescent mind-set. Together these two ingredients make for a pushy, in-your-face pet.

Another cause for pushy behavior in a cat can be breed-related. Certain breeds simply are pushier than others. A Siamese, for example, may require almost constant attention on your part, whereas a Persian may be quite content to spend most of the day alone, with barely any need for your attention. In general, the Oriental breeds tend to be more demonstrative than other breeds. They include:

◆ Abyssinian
◆ Siamese
◆ Burmese
◆ Tonkinese
◆ Balinese
◆ Javanese
◆ Oriental
◆ Singapura
◆ Somali
◆ Colorpoint shorthair

Choosing one of these breeds will almost guarantee a more active pet, with a strong desire to be in on all that goes on in your home. This is not necessarily a bad thing; many owners actually prefer this almost doglike personality, preferring the attentive, unrestrained nature of the Oriental breeds to that of the more reserved ones.

Some cats learn to become pushy and rude through the unintentional actions of their owners. For instance, if your young kitten happens to jump up onto the dinner table while you are eating, what will he learn if you not only allow the behavior but also reward it with a tidbit from your dish? Or what would your cat learn if every time he jumped up into your lap and meowed plaintively you stroked him lavishly, then got up and fed him dinner? In this way, you can take a normal cat and turn him into a pushy brat, who knows that he can get what he wants just by vocalizing, jumping up, nagging, or bullying you in some way, much as a spoiled child might do in the supermarket when wanting his parent to buy him some candy. The parent who gives in just to avoid a tantrum from the child only serves to reinforce the obnoxious behavior.

SOLUTION

Try not to encourage unwanted behavior, right from the start. If your kitten begins to jump up onto you or the table when he isn't allowed to, pick him up, place him down on the floor, and say, "*No!*" in a firm voice. If he continues to do so, give him a squirt of water from your trusty spray bottle. Above all, do not reward any behavior you think undesirable; the last thing you should do when your cat becomes pushy is give him a pat on the head or a treat.

Sometimes consistently ignoring a cat's unwanted behavior will be enough to put a stop to it. For instance, if your cat sits in front of you while you are reading and begins to plaintively meow over and over again in an attempt to get you to feed him or let him out, completely ignore him and see what happens. Eventually he should give up and walk away. He may try it again several times, but if each time you ignore him, odds are the behavior will stop, because it isn't being encouraged in any way. Try this if the pushy behavior isn't unbearable or too serious.

Another technique that can work well on the pushy cat is redirecting the behavior. Often your cat may appear pushy or troublesome due to sheer boredom or a lack of attention on your part. Instead of waiting for the cat to behave in an undesirable manner, try giving him something to do that will satisfy his need for stimulation. Buy a cat teaser toy at your local pet store and use it to stimulate your cat at least three or four times par day. Leave a few toys down on the floor. Get the cat a multitiered, carpeted cat play structure. Even a cardboard box filled with newspaper and a few treats can be enough to redirect your pushy cat's behavior and give him an avenue for all that energy and desire.

ROAMING

DESCRIPTION

If your cat is allowed access to the outdoors he may roam up to several blocks away from home to survey his territory. Even neutered cats, both male and female, will participate in this behavior, though unneutered males will roam the farthest and stay away the longest. Typically, the cat will not travel farther than a few blocks from home. When measured in a radius from the home, however, this area become quite large and may include busy streets, yards with dogs, and other cats, who rarely take kindly to another cat's intrusions.

The cat who roams will often stay out all day and come home around dinnertime. Often he will have scratches or bite marks from run-ins with other cats. The roaming cat will tend to be somewhat less social with guests and other pets than a cat raised indoors. Odds are your outdoor cat won't be as willing to be handled, even by you. By being allowed to roam all day he enters into a mind-set much closer to that of his wild cousins, one that requires a much more independent way of thinking and acting.

WHY YOUR CAT IS DOING THIS

Roaming is a normal behavior for any cat allowed access to the outside. As males tend to covet their territories somewhat more vigorously than females, they will most likely range farther and stay away longer, especially if unneutered. The reason is simple: your cat wants to exercise his territorial instincts, which tell him that he needs to procure mates and food. The larger the territory, the more mates and prey will be available. The ranges of domesticated cats tend to be on the small side, however, at least when compared to cats in the wild, due to the density of the cat population in urban, suburban, and rural locales.

Unneutered cats are particularly apt to roam far from home and will have an overwhelming desire to mate with other cats. Proof of this can be found in any pet shelter in the country; thousands upon thousands of unwanted kittens and cats, produced through the mating of unneutered roamers, go homeless, and end up euthanized each year. Countless owners bring unwanted litters of kittens into shelters, thinking that a home awaits for these cuddly little creatures. Unfortunately, most of them are destroyed within three to five days. The cavalier attitudes of many cat owners who refuse to have their outdoor cats neutered is the number-one cause of this tragedy.

Cats allowed to roam become injured much more frequently than those kept indoors. Cars, dogs, infectious diseases, and fights with other cats all contribute to a much higher mortality rate among outdoor cats. The life-threatening diseases that can be passed from cat to cat include:

◆ Feline Immunodeficiency Virus (FIV)
◆ Feline Infectious Anemia

- ◆ Feline Infectious Peritonitis (FIP)
- ◆ Feline Leukemia (FeLV)
- ◆ Feline Panleukopenia
- ◆ Feline Respiratory Disease Complex (FRDC)
- ◆ Feline Urologic Syndrome (FUS)
- ◆ Rabies

In addition, outdoor cats routinely become infected with external parasites, which can sicken the pet and cause all manner of medical problems, as well as skin and coat diseases.

SOLUTION

The first step to prevent roaming is having your cat neutered. Doing so (if you haven't already) will dramatically reduce your cat's desire to patrol his territory and search for appropriate mates. Far fewer cat fights will occur, as will nose-to-nose meetings of potential combatants. This will reduce your cat's chances of infection as well as the number of injuries he sustains. If you insist on allowing your cat access to the outdoors, you simply must neuter him, for his safety and for the good of the species. In addition, be sure to have your cat inoculated for all of the aforementioned infectious diseases, particularly if you intend on allowing him out of the home.

The best solution to the problem of roaming is keeping your cat inside all the time. Indoor-only cats live on average nearly five years longer than their outdoor counterparts, due to the absence of so many potentially fatal factors in their lives. Most outdoor cats, in addition to the threats of dogs, cars, parasites, disease, and other cats, often develop arthritis and other joint disorders much sooner than indoor pets. As debilitating joint pain is a big cause of euthanasia among older cats, it stands to reason that allowing your cat outside will significantly lessen his overall quality of life.

For those who feel that their cats need to experience the outdoors on some level, there are options. First, consider screening in a porch or deck and allowing your cat easy access to it, perhaps through a small cat door. Or you could build a cat run on the side of the home, fenced in with chicken wire and accessed from the home through a small window or cat door. If you do so, be sure to fence the top as well, to prevent escape and to keep other cats out. Using an enclosed area will give your cat access to the outside while removing many of its potential threats (excluding infectious diseases and parasites). Many pet stores now sell prefab cat runs that take only minutes to assemble and install; if the logistics of your home will allow this type of structure, consider it as a safer option to letting your cat wander on his own.

Another option is teaching your cat, from early kittenhood, to walk on a leash and harness. Commonly taught to cats by trainers worldwide, the behavior must be started early on for it to be accepted by the cat. Adult cats rarely take to the restrictive feeling of the harness and leash and often panic. For this reason, be careful trying this with an adult cat.

To begin, you first need to purchase a harness for your kitten. Fitting around the cat's chest, the harness is essential, as few cats will tolerate any pressure at all on a collar fastened around their necks. The leash, attached to the harness, is almost imperceptible to the cat, as any pressure from it is spread out over a wide area of the pet's midsection.

After purchasing the harness, the next step is acclimating your kitten to wearing it. Start out placing it on the kitten for a very short time, perhaps only a minute or two. With each passing day increase the time he wears it until, after a few weeks, he is comfortable wearing it for at least thirty minutes. During and after these sessions, be sure to reward the kitten with treats and praise.

Once your kitten is acclimated to the harness, clip a very thin, light leash to it and allow him to drag it around for a few minutes, just to get used to its weight. Take care not to let the leash get caught on anything, however, as this could cause your kitten to get hurt or panick. Gradually increase the time he has the leash clipped on until it can be connected for thirty minutes with no objections. Again, reward and praise him. Be sure all of this training occurs in the home.

Next, pick up the leash and follow the kitten around the home for a few minutes. Let him dictate where you go. Every now and then gradually increase tension on the leash, to get him used to the idea. Eventually, you should be able to begin gently steering him in the direction you choose. Encourage him with treats and praise, and be as upbeat as you can.

Once you reach this stage, take the kitten out into a quiet, fenced-in yard and allow him to explore. Follow him around, but keep hold of the leash. Let him walk around for ten minutes or so, then pick him up and go back inside. These outdoor sessions can increase in time to thirty minutes or more; just be sure to keep hold of the leash, meant not to control but to simply prevent escape. If started early, most cat will accept this controlled method of outdoor exploration.

SCRATCHING FURNITURE

DESCRIPTION

Many cat owners suffer from this expensive cat behavior, which often results in damage to valuable pieces of furniture in the home, particularly sofas and chairs. The scratching usually occurs on upholstered furniture, especially pieces with highly textured fabrics, which cats seem to prefer, as their claws grip these surfaces better. Fabric and wood become marred, ripped, and destroyed, requiring refinishing, reupholstering, or replacement.

WHY YOUR CAT IS DOING THIS

Scratching is a normal and necessary behavior that all cats must exhibit to stay happy and healthy. The behavior allows your cat to accomplish several things. First, the outer layers of her claws need to be shed on a regular basis, in order to keep them sharp. Scratching them against an appropriate surface helps this process along. Second, scratching is a marking behavior, along with spraying, fecal marking, and scent depositing, meant to establish the boundaries of a cat's territory. Other cats, upon seeing the scratch marks, understand that they are about to encroach on another feline's territory. Some scent from small glands in your cat's paws is also deposited during the act, underlining the "keep out" message.

In addition, the scratching, which often occurs right after your cat wakes up from a nap, helps her stretch out her sleepy muscles. The act is similar to our stretching our arms to our sides after rising in the morning.

Unneutered cats, both male and female, will tend to scratch more than their counterparts. In addition, males tend to scratch more than females, as they have larger territories and guard them more ardently.

SOLUTION

Rather than ending this behavior, you should choose to redirect it to an area where scratching is acceptable to you. Your cat needs to scratch; the question simply becomes an issue of where.

First, go out and purchase several quality scratching posts, if you haven't already. Don't get small, thin, wimpy ones; instead, make sure they are at least two to three feet high and eight to ten inches wide, to provide your cat with ample scratching surface while she is in a stretched-out, nearly vertical position. Choose scratching posts covered with a rough, "scratchable" surface, such as wrapped hemp cord or thick carpet. Locate them around the home, near wherever she tends to take catnaps, as the waking up period is the most likely time for scratching. Actually show her the new scratching posts and scratch at them yourself, so she can model the behavior.

A multitiered "kitty condo," a carpeted, jungle gym type apparatus that cats love to sleep, climb, and play on, can be obtained at a good pet store. Carpeted, these tall structures will also act as additional scratching posts for your cat.

Having your cat neutered will reduce the amount of scratch-marking she does around the home. Without the hormonal pressure to establish and defend a territory, she will scratch only to shed nail coverings and to stretch out after napping.

If you do catch your cat scratching at the furniture despite her being provided with acceptable scratching posts, give her a squirt of water from a plant sprayer bottle while she is in the act. As you do so, say, *"No!"* in a firm voice. When she makes the choice to use the scratching posts, praise her lavishly and consider rewarding her with a small treat.

To prevent your cat from scratching the furniture when you are away, apply strips of double-sided tape to the areas she is most likely to scratch. The sticky texture will be unpleasant to her paws and will send her elsewhere, hopefully to the preferred posts. Keep using this technique for several weeks, whenever you are away. Once she begins to regularly used the scratching posts instead of the furniture, you can consider removing the tape.

SEPARATION ANXIETY

DESCRIPTION

Though separation anxiety is nowhere near as common a problem in cats as in dogs, felines can and do suffer from separation anxiety when apart from their owners or from other pets in the home. The cat who suffers during times of separation can show destructive behavior and may vocalize excessively, to the point of disturbing neighbors. In addition, your lonely cat may redirect his anxiety into activities such as grooming and overgroom himself to the point of causing hair loss or skin disorders. He might also lose much of his appetite and lose substantial amounts of weight or even stop using the litter box.

WHY YOUR CAT IS DOING THIS

Several causes might be at work in the cat suffering from separation anxiety. First, cats acquired well before their eighth week of life are much more likely to show signs of this problem, as they were not allowed to experience the full amount of socialization necessary to create a stable social mind-set. When a five-

or six-week-old kitten goes home with a new owner, the pet tends to bond very closely to that person, so close, in fact, that the absence of that owner, even for a short period of time, can create great emotional stress for the cat. Bottle-fed orphans are particularly susceptible to the problem, as the owner becomes the surrogate mother, someone the cat cannot seem to be without for too long.

Certain cat breeds can exhibit separation anxiety more than others. The Oriental breeds are much more likely to do so, as they tend to be more interactive than other breeds. These breeds include the Abyssinian, Balinese, Burmese, Havana Brown, Cornish Rex, Devon Rex, Siamese, Sphynx, and Tonkinese. All have a very social persona and don't do well left alone for long periods.

Some cats who exhibit profound separation anxiety simply have a hereditary predisposition toward the behavior. With these cats, the fear of isolation seems to have been programmed into their personalities. When this is the case, modifying the behavior becomes extremely difficult.

SOLUTION

Once a cat has exhibited profound separation anxiety, it is difficult to modify the behavior. Techniques worth trying include having a friend or neighbor stop by the home once each day while you are gone to interact with the cat for at least a few minutes. Doing so can help forestall some or all of the symptoms of the problem, particularly the destructive behavior, often evidenced by marred or ripped furniture, or improper elimination habits, particularly urinating out of the litter box.

As is the case with many behavioral problems, try making your cat's environment as exciting as possible by putting down numerous cat toys, leaving a newspaper-filled cardboard box down on the floor, hiding treats around the home, and leaving a radio or television on while you are gone. Some owners will even purchase a pet video tape and play it for their cats while they are gone. These videos, available at many pet stores, show cats, dogs, or other animals on the screen, in a size that appears most lifelike to your cat. The shapes and movements seen by him can often act as a great distraction, keeping him from worrying too much about being alone.

The best way to deal with feline separation anxiety is to avoid it from the beginning. First, if you know you are going to be gone for ten to twelve hours each day be sure to avoid getting the Oriental breeds mentioned earlier, particularly the Siamese. These cats insist on having regular companionship and are nearly doglike in nature. Breeds that deal well with being alone all day include:

- ◆ American shorthair
- ◆ American wirehair
- ◆ British shorthair
- ◆ Bombay
- ◆ Chartreux
- ◆ Egyptian Mau

- ◆ Exotic
- ◆ Korat
- ◆ Maine Coon cat
- ◆ Manx
- ◆ Persian
- ◆ Russian Blue
- ◆ Scottish Fold

Avoiding a breed with a predisposition for separation anxiety will help prevent the behavior, though not having one of the aforementioned breeds certainly won't be the end of the world. After all, cat breeds are not nearly as diverse in temperament as are dog breeds.

Another way to minimize the problem is to get two kittens instead of one, right from the start. Regardless of the breed, the two littermates will amuse themselves all day and won't worry about you and your whereabouts. Just be sure not to take them home until they are at least eight weeks old.

Choose your cat wisely; always pick the kitten who seems curious and confident yet not overbearing. Never choose the shrinking violet in the corner, just because you feel sorry for him or her. You might end up with an insecure, timid pet who can't stand to be without you.

STEALING

DESCRIPTION

Some cats get into the habit of stealing food left out on the table or counter or articles of clothing left on the bedroom floor or on a chair or bureau top. The food will invariably be eaten; the article of clothing will often be chewed or suckled upon until it becomes unusable.

WHY YOUR CAT IS DOING THIS

As far as the food theft is concerned, she is stealing food for the simple reason that she is hungry and it is there for the taking. Theft of clothing (particularly socks and underwear) occurs for the same reason that cats choose to chew on fabrics (see "Chewing, Fabric and Clothing"). Your thief loves the scent and taste of your body and takes the errant sock or pair of underwear to a safe hiding place so she can chew and suckle on it to her heart's content. This seemingly odd behavior occurs often in cats weaned at too early an age; your thieving little feline seems to need to continue the nursing act into adulthood and chooses an article of your clothing because you are the closest thing to Mommy. The scent on the article reminds your cat of you; mouthing it comforts her.

Stealing an article of clothing and chewing on it

can also occur in teething kittens, who need to chew on something to help relieve the pain. When nothing else is available, your kitten will choose whatever feels best in her mouth.

SOLUTION

Ending food theft is simple; simply keep all tables and countertops free of edible items. Also, if your cat is getting into drawers or cupboards, install baby-proof locks on them (see "Garbage or Cupboard Raiding"). Be sure that she is receiving the proper amount of food each day, as underfed cats will often search out food in other places to satisfy their appetites.

Stopping the theft of articles of clothing shouldn't be that hard, either. First, be sure never to leave clothes on the floor or out in the open. All dirty items should be placed in a clothes hamper, located in an area where the cat cannot gain access. Provide your cat with soft cat toys that she can chew on; try to purchase ones that approximate the same texture and feel as the articles of clothing she once stole. Also, be sure to handle these toys each day to get your scent on them. This will make her more likely to accept them. In addition, let her know you approve of her chewing on the toys by using them in a keep-away or fetch game. Tease her a bit with the toy, then let her have it.

If the sock or underwear thefts continue, try spraying a sock with soapy water or dabbing it with a little Tabasco sauce. Then leave it down on the floor for the cat to steal. After getting a taste, she probably won't repeat the act anytime soon.

If your kitten is teething, expect her to chew on something. Provide her with toys designed especially for teething kittens. Available at your local pet store, these toys will have just the right feel and texture to help relieve the teething pain.

TIMIDITY
(SEE "HIDING.")

UNDERACTIVE BEHAVIOR

DESCRIPTION

Your underactive cat doesn't seem to move around as much as she once might have and may now refrain from playing, jumping, or interacting. She might show fluctuations in her weight and might or might not be more vocal than usual. Dry coat and skin might also develop. Your underactive cat may also sleep more than usual and be lethargic when awake. Also, she might appear more impatient or irritable and could even show an exaggerated sensitivity to touch.

WHY YOUR CAT IS DOING THIS

Several factors could be causing your cat's underactive behavior. First, an uncommon condition called *hypothyroidism* could be developing. As a result of a severe reduction in the production of hormones by the cat's thyroid gland, her metabolism slows down. A hypothyroid condition will also cause your cat to gain weight. She might sleep more and develop skin and coat problems, particularly dry, brittle fur, and itchy skin.

Advancing age will have a slowing effect on your cat's behavior as well. Old age slows her metabolism and causes her to sleep more. Aching joints may limit her ability to move, jump, and play and cause her to be more irritable. Her appetite could fluctuate, as could her weight, which often increases with age, due to the slowing metabolism.

Injury or illness can also be a major cause of underactive feline behavior. Cats tend not to broadcast their aches and pains and instead choose to lay low and stay quiet. This stoic attitude often blinds us to the presence of a serious condition. Injured or sick cats, in addition to being inactive, will lose their appetite and be extremely sensitive to touch.

SOLUTION

The very first step in dealing with an underactive cat is a trip to the veterinarian. The doctor will be able to determine if your cat has an underactive thyroid gland or if illness or injury might be the culprit. If old age is the cause, the veterinarian will be able to determine that as well and also give advice on how to deal with it, including dietary changes and rearrangement of cat's environment to better suit her flagging physical capabilities (see "Old Age, Behavior Problems Related To").

If the problem is being caused by an underactive thyroid gland, you will have to give your cat medication every day to counteract the deficiency. Once she is on the synthetic hormones, her activity levels and overall health will return to normal.

If the sluggish behavior is due to illness or injury, try to determine how it occurred. Is your cat allowed outside each day? If so, she might have contracted an illness from another cat. If the problem is due to an injury, was the injury received during a territorial dispute with another outdoor cat? If so, you might consider bringing your cat indoors on a full-time basis to prevent reinjury.

VETERINARIAN, FEAR OF

DESCRIPTION

Many cat owners know the drill; take your cat in to the veterinarian for his annual checkup and then watch the fireworks. Most cats react badly to the poking and prodding that a veterinarian must do to fully examine the pet. The cat's temperature is taken, blood may be drawn, and his ears and mouth must be looked into. All of this is highly humiliating to most cats; some simply won't sit still, causing the veterinarian and his or her assistants to have to don heavy gloves and immobilize the cat to facilitate the exam. As this may be the only level of contact he and the veterinarian ever experiences, you can begin to understand why the mere sight of the clinic might set your cat off.

Many cats will resist the probing and restraining and try to extricate themselves from the situation. When unsuccessful, some will reluctantly accede while others will scream, claw, bite, and hiss. Most cats fall somewhere in between, causing veterinarians to often get a real workout.

WHY YOUR CAT IS DOING THIS

Let's face it: from your cat's point of view, the veterinarian is an evil, controlling bully, hell-bent on causing embarrassment and pain. Your cat is by nature a very independent soul, who resists at every turn anyone's attempt to control or restrain him. He also does not feel at all comfortable with a total stranger taking such physical liberties and, quite naturally, resists. When the veterinarian continues, however, your cat begins to fear the situation and can often slip into a "fight or flight" mode. He cannot run away, though, as he is being held securely, so he tries to fight his way to freedom. Even that usually fails, leaving him to surrender to the moment.

Cats have remarkable memories. If someone accidentally (or otherwise) hurts a cat, the pet may retain that forever and never feel at ease around that person again. Such is the lot of the veterinarian. He or she, in trying to examine and treat the cat, must create an unbearably humiliating and scary situation for the cat, who may retain the memory and forever resist the veterinarian's wishes, no matter how careful and gentle he or she is.

SOLUTION

We simply must try to make the veterinarian's life a bit easier. But how? One way to do it is to handle our cats each and every day, starting in early kittenhood. From the very first day, you should regularly pick your cat up, examine his body, look into his ears and mouth, and check his coat and skin for parasites. Brush and comb him frequently, and after each handling or grooming session give him a delicious treat as a reward. By desensitizing him to examination from a very early age you will be making your veterinarian's job much easier. Doing so will help you keep your feline in the best shape possible.

If your cat already hates going to the veterinarian, there isn't much that can be done except to attempt to alter his opinion of the place. Try visiting the veterinarian's office every now and then for a "nonvisit"; simply take your cat in for a quick "hello" from the staff there, who can (if time allows) pet your cat and give him treats. You can even play a short tease game with him, right there in the office. Take his favorite teaser toy with you and get him to chase it back and forth for a minute. Praise and reward him, then leave.

If the staff at the clinic is tolerant of you doing this, it will help to at least partially defuse the cat's fears of going there.

Some cats become so fear-aggressive that they must be sedated in order to be examined. If this is the case with your cat, ask your veterinarian to prescribe a mild sedative that the cat can be given before the visit. Normally provided in pill form, the sedative will calm the cat down enough to allow the exam to take place.

PART THREE

The Ten Most Important Ways to Minimize Feline Behavioral Problems

This last section provides you with the ten most valuable measures you can take to ensure a trouble-free cat and a great pet/owner relationship. Meant to be fast and easy to read and reread, each of the ten "commandments" will be about a page in length. They will aid owners in preventing major and minor feline behavioral problems and help strengthen the bond between owner and pet. Take some time now to go over each one carefully, so you can begin applying them to your cat right away.

1. SCHEDULE A YEARLY VISIT TO YOUR VETERINARIAN

Every cat should make at least one trip to the veterinarian each year, to receive an overall examination and to be administered the proper immunizations. In addition, your veterinarian should be allowed to become as familiar as possible with your cat, to allow him or her the ability to compare your pet's appearance and behavior over time. Being able to do so is a valuable diagnostic tool for the doctor, who may be able to notice a subtle change in behavior or appearance better than you. Weight gain, for instance, often occurs too slowly for many owners to notice. To the veterinarian, however, the gain will be obvious.

When visiting the veterinarian, try to carry your cat in a sturdy cat carrier, available at all pet stores. Doing so will protect her from other pets in the waiting room and help keep her calm. If your cat is ill or injured, try to have as much information as possible available for the veterinarian. Be accurate with the symptoms or with the details of the accident, if your cat was hurt in some way.

Remember that of all the individuals involved in your cat's life, the veterinarian is, next to you, the most important. He or she may spot a serious medical problem before it has a chance to adversely affect your cat's health and behavior. The veterinarian can also give you sound advice on behavior and even on areas such as diet, breeding, training, and pet selection. Keeping in touch with your veterinarian is one of the best ways known to help minimize all manner of cat problems, so, don't be shy!

2. NEVER HIT OR ABUSE YOUR CAT IN ANY WAY

Though this directive may sound obvious to all who read it, cat abuse remains one of the major causes of feline behavioral problems today. Smacking or kicking a cat in an effort to get him or her to stop some undesirable behavior will not only result in a permanent breakdown of the cat/owner relationship but can cause serious or fatal injury to the pet as well, whose small body cannot possibly hold up to being struck by a human being ten times his size.

More cats are hurt or killed by human beings each year than by dogs. The tragedy of this statement is that, as humans, we have a choice not to harm a small creature but often do nonetheless, out of either frustration and anger or some hard-to-define sadistic rationale. Unlike canines, who bite human beings thousands of times each year, cats rarely inflict serious harm on us, except for the occasional bite or scratch, more often than not given during a defensive moment. They won't hurt anyone unless confronted in some way or made to think that their lives are threatened.

Cats react poorly to not only blatant physical abuse but verbal abuse as well. Yelling and screaming doesn't work well on cats, who will become extremely stressed at your tirade and in all likelihood exhibit additional behavior problems as a result. The cat's world is a relatively quiet one (Siamese cats excluded), another reason we like them so much as pets. For us to scream at one is contrary to everything they are and to the very reasons we choose them to share our homes.

Those who use force on a cat to alter an undesirable behavior show a true ignorance of feline behavior and defeat the very purpose of having a cat in the first place. Cat owners keep cats not only for companionship but also for their beauty, physical prowess, elegance, and independent nature. Owning a cat is much like befriending a great work of art. Why would you want to abuse such a thing of beauty when there are so many better, more intelligent, humane ways to alter a simple behavioral problem? Use your mind and your heart, instead of your foot.

3. READ AS MANY BOOKS AND MAGAZINES ON CAT BEHAVIOR AS POSSIBLE

Knowledge of feline behavior and physiology changes and increases every day. As a cat owner, you should attempt to keep up with these changes as best you can for the sake of your cat and for your own curiosity. In addition, new products designed specifically with the cat in mind come onto the market every day; many might be of great value to you in your attempts to maintain a good relationship with your cat.

Take a trip to your local bookstore and take a look at just how many cat-related books are offered. Topics range far and wide and include information on breeds, behavior, new trends, diet, medicine, toys, and a host of other important categories. You can learn what the experts have to say about your specific breed of cat, learn about a new breed, or even find out how to teach your cat tricks. With the rising popularity of cats all over the world, available information on them has been increasing dramatically. To keep up, consider checking the bookshelves at your local bookstore.

For the most current information on cats, check out the magazine racks. Today more than a half-dozen cat magazines are available for you to buy. As magazines come out on a monthly basis, they are better able to keep up with the latest cat trends than books, which often take months or even years to go from finished manuscript to bookshelf. Cat magazines will give you good information on all aspects of cat ownership and will also help put you in touch with breeders in your area, if you are in the market for a specific type of cat. Great articles on nutrition, health, and behavior, provide regular, invaluable additions to your cat "IQ."

Reading up on your particular breed of cat will help you understand her better and might aid you in setting up her perfect environment. Knowing that your Siamese needs more socialization than a Persian, for instance, might convince you to spend more time with her or to at least get a friend to stop in to visit with the cat while you are gone at work. Breed-specific books and magazine articles can also alert you to specific medical or anatomical conditions that might uniquely affect your breed. Owning a hairless Sphynx, for example, would require you to guard your pet from direct sunlight, which can give this breed a bad sunburn.

By staying as informed as possible about all things cat, you will be better prepared to deal with any problems that might pop up in your own cat's life. Plus, you might learn something new about your favorite feline pet!

4. TEACH YOUR CAT A NEW BEHAVIOR ONCE EACH MONTH

Cats are intelligent, thinking animals who learn something new each day, usually on their own. Many owners neglect the intelligence of their felines, however, and assume that they are perfectly happy to go through the same routines every day, without any new challenges or problems to solve.

Not true! Cats have always been masterful thinkers; all predators have to be, if they are to survive. Your cat is no different. She can easily learn new behaviors, if you have the patience to teach her. By teaching her one new behavior each month you will help her expand her mind and learn to think, instead of just react to her environment. Most cats are never very intellectually stimulated, because their owners do not tend to think of them in those terms. Owners assume that only dogs are trainable, not the more independent-minded cat.

Teach your cat at least one new behavior each month to keep her mentally active and happy. It can be something as simple as finding a treat inside a box filled with newspaper or learning that a ringing bell means dinner is served. You can teach her to sit on command, use a cat door, or even wave at you. To learn how to teach her some easy tricks, go to your library or bookstore and select a trick-training book for cats. In it you will learn how to teach a multitude of tricks and behaviors to your curious and intelligent cat. Remember that she doesn't have to learn anything; it is all optional and meant to expand her mind.

Tricks aren't the only things you can teach your cat. By hiding delicious treats in different locations around the home encourage her to better utilize her fine sense of smell. Or teach her to sleep in a special spot on or near your bed. The possibilities are limited only by your imagination!

5. KEEP YOUR CAT'S ENVIRONMENT AS INTERESTING AND SAFE AS POSSIBLE

Providing your cat with a fun, secure home life will go a long way in stimulating her mind, prolonging her life, and preventing bad behaviors. First, always have a number of fun toys available for her, including stuffed mice, teasers, catnip-filled yarn balls, and wind-up or battery-powered toys. Old reliable, toys such as crumpled balls of newspaper and Ping-Pong balls also work well. Be sure to initiate regular play sessions with her, to stimulate her mind and body and to help strengthen the bond between you both.

Provide your cat with at least two scratching posts, to satisfy her need to scratch, sharpen her claws, and stretch her body out after napping. Also, consider purchasing a carpeted, multitiered "kitty condo" or jungle gym, which will provide your cat with hours of fun, exercise, and a feeling of security. Leave a radio on every now and then, tuned to a talk station, to create the illusion of someone being home. Just be sure to keep it low, so as not to hurt your cat's excellent sense of hearing.

Be sure to remove all potentially toxic substances from your cat's domain, to preserve her health. Cleaners, solvents, motor oil, antifreeze, and any other poisonous materials should be safely stored away in a lockable cupboard. In addition, be sure to remove from your cat's environment any toxic house-or garden plants (see "Plant Eating"), which can cause severe illness or even death, if the cat is not treated promptly.

6. AVOID ALLOWING YOUR CAT OUTDOORS

The argument over giving domestic cats access to the outdoors for extended periods of time has staunch supporters on both sides of the issue. Supporters of the practice claim that cats need to be allowed to go outside in order to express their wild instincts. A cat wouldn't be a cat, they argue, without the ability to stalk, explore, and interact with nature. Restricting a cat to a small home or apartment, they say, is cruel.

Others see it differently and recognize that the decision to own a cat implies a certain tacit cooperation with the very idea of domesticity, which by its nature restricts an animal's ability to express certain intact instincts. We domesticate a cat, dog, horse, or hamster to harness its innate skills and apply them to some task, such as mousing, retrieving ducks from a pond, or transporting us from one place to another, or just enjoy its company.

By owning a cat you change her relationship with nature. She no longer must hunt to live. Instead, you feed her. She need not breed or seek out shelter from the elements. Again, you provide everything. She eliminates in a box, instead of a pile of dirt in the woods. Why is it perfectly acceptable to change those aspects of the feline lifestyle while at the same time abhor another adaptation of domesticity, namely, keeping the cat indoors? The cat's "nature" has already been corrupted by the trappings (and advantages) of domesticity. Why be adamant about this one point?

Though the romantic appeal of a cat running free is not lost on me, the logic used by these outdoors advocates is. After all, the same persons who support allowing cats to roam freely never seem to award the same rights to canines, who certainly have just as rich a history of survival in the wild as do felines. If dogs can cope, why not allow them the same freedoms? And what about the hamster? Shouldn't it be allowed to scurry freely through fields of wheat, waiting anxiously for the moment when the hawks will come?

The answer, I believe, is that many cat owners simply do not want to define the cat as a domestic creature and cannot let go of the idea of the cat being a wild, mystical "visitor" to the world of humans. Whether this is the case I am not sure, but I do know that cats are not as invincible and ethereal as some of us would like to believe.

With regard to keeping a cat in such a small territory, your feline will adapt to nearly any size domain, provided she has enough food, little or no competition, ample companionship, and adequate mental stimulation. Place three or four cats in a studio apartment and that would be crowded. But keeping one or two neutered cats in a home or apartment certainly does not pose a problem, provided all needs are met. As long as the cats are raised from kittenhood in this territory, they will accept it as their own and be happy with it. The problems arise when cats raised outdoors most of their lives are suddenly thrust into a much smaller territory, with much fewer stimuli, relatively speaking. Even this pet can over time, however, come to accept the smaller domain, provided the owner supplies him or her with enough mental stimulation.

You as a responsible cat owner must make the decision whether or not to allow your pet access to the outdoors. My advice is to keep your pet inside from kittenhood on, making sure that her home is as mentally challenging as possible (see commandment #5). If you simply cannot agree with this, create an enclosed area for your cat to play in once each day or teach her to walk on a leash and harness. Either option will allow the cat access to the outdoors in a controlled, safe manner and prevent disease, injury, or death from destroying your relationship.

If you still insist on allowing your cat access to the outdoors, at least have her neutered and properly inoculated. Doing both will prevent euthanization of unwanted kittens and minimize the risk of her contracting a fatal feline disease.

7. NEUTER YOUR CAT

This one is really a no-brainer. If you are not a professional breeder, then you have no reason to avoid having your cat neutered by a competent veterinarian. Castration for the male and spaying for the female are both simple surgeries that cost little (usually about fifty dollars for castration and seventy-five to eighty dollars for spaying) and can only improve the cat's demeanor. The drive to mate will be removed and the territorial instinct minimized. Plus, the chance of unwanted kittens being produced will be eliminated. Spraying, fecal marking, fighting, excess scratching, roaming, and dominance issues will all be dramatically reduced or ended. You will be left with a happy, personable pet, who will live longer and be statistically less likely to contract numerous forms of cancer.

Having the procedure done at around the seventh month of life will ensure that your cat has time to develop properly, both physically and mentally. Even cats neutered as young kittens make great pets, however, though they do tend to remain in a more "kittenish" state of mind all their lives. Adult cats can also be neutered effectively, though the beneficial effects the procedure has on behavior may take several months to surface.

8. MINIMIZE ABRUPT CHANGES IN YOUR CAT'S LIFE

Your cat will fare much better behaviorally if you do your best to keep the status quo, with regard to household routines as well as the actual physical environment. Cats love routine; they get very comfortable with having you come home at the same time each day and with seeing the same goings-on through the living room window. Your cat will grow accustomed to the furniture (and its arrangement) in your home, to the carpet, to the smell of your bedspread, and even to the brand of air freshener you use. When you abruptly change things in his environment, he might react adversely to it, often by exhibiting some unacceptable behavior, including house-training mishaps and destructiveness.

The trick to keeping your cat happy in his environment is to either keep things the same or else change them gradually enough so that he doesn't notice. For instance, if you need to change the type of food he is eating, do so over a two- or three-week period, slowly reducing the amount of the old food while replacing it with the new. Doing so will prevent the cat from objecting to the change and prevent any digestive problems from the switch.

Try to stick with the same brand of cat litter as well. Changing litter may just be the biggest cause of house-training mishaps, so, if at all possible, stay with old reliable. If you must switch, do so using the same gradual method you'd use with a food switch. Taking at least two to three weeks to change over should prevent any problems.

Moving to a new home will often throw a cat for a loop, so be prepared for behavioral changes in your cat. To minimize them, consider restricting your cat to one room for a few days before giving him free rein in the home. Put his litter box in one corner and his food and water dishes in another. After he gets used to the scent of the new place, give him access to the rest of the home and watch him closely. After a few days he should be fine.

Remember: change things gradually, in order to preserve your cat's well-being. Doing so will ease your cat into the new situation and prevent the undesirable behaviors that often accompany changes in a cat's territory.

9. BE SURE YOUR CAT WEARS A SAFE COLLAR WITH A SUITABLE IDENTIFICATION TAG

Nothing hurts more than losing a beloved cat. Unfortunately, it happens all the time. Besides having your cat neutered, the best way to prevent this heartache is to make sure your cat wears a collar with an identification tag firmly attached. The collar itself needs to be made of an elastic material, so that if it is snagged on a branch or fence top the cat won't choke. These stretchable cat collars are available at most pet stores and come in different sizes to fit any cat. The identification tag, also available through pet shops, should have your telephone number on it. Provided with this information, any Good Samaritan who finds your feline will be able to return her to you. Without it, your cat could end up in a shelter, where she could very well be euthanized within days. Give her a fair chance to be returned safely; make sure she wears a collar and identification tag.

10. LOVE YOUR CAT

When it all comes right down to it, we own cats because of the companionship and love we feel for them and from them. A silent understanding should exist between owner and pet, one in which each knows the care and concern felt by the other. Both pet and owner feed off of these feelings, making both feel wanted and secure.

Perhaps no piece of cat advice is more important than for you to love your pet, unconditionally, despite whatever behavioral problems might pop up. When your cat feels true love coming from you, she will sense a stability and strength in the relationship, which will in turn calm her and help prevent future behavioral problems from occurring. A well-adjusted, happy cat will be far less likely to act out than an abused, unloved animal. By openly caring for her you will do more to prevent problem behavior than all the pet books in the world combined. And besides, it'll make you a happier, better behaved person, too!

APPENDIXES

Appendix A

NATIONAL CAT ASSOCIATIONS AND ORGANIZATIONS

American Cat Association
8101 Katherine Avenue
Panorama City, CA 91402
(818) 781-5656

American Cat Fancier's Association
PO Box 203
Point Lookout, MO 65726
(417) 334-5430

American Society for the Prevention of Cruelty to Animals (ASPCA)
1755 Massachusetts Avenue NW, Suite 418
Washington, DC 20036
(202) 232-5020

Canadian Cat Association
220 Advance Boulevard, Suite 101
Brampton, Ontario,
Canada L6T 4J5
(905) 459-1481

Cat Fancier's Federation
PO Box 661
Gratis, OH 45330
(513) 787-9009

The Humane Society
2100 L Street NW
Washington, DC 20037
(202) 452-1100
(see also local listings)

Appendix B

MAGAZINES AND WEB SITES OF INTEREST

Magazines:

Cat Fancy Magazine
Box 6050
Mission Viejo, CA 92690
www.catfancy.com

Cats and Kittens
Pet Business, Inc.
7-L Dundas Circle
Greensboro, NC 27407
www.catsandkittens.com

Cats Magazine
Primedia
260 Madison Avenue
NY, NY 10016
www.catsmag.com

Web sites:

www.4cats.com
A complete Web guide, directing you to all your needs.

www.healthypets.com
A great site for health tips on your cat.

www.internetpets.com
A complete online pet store.

www.kittencare.com
Supplies, and advice, including behavioral advice.

www.petopia.com
A complete pet Web site.

www.pets.com
Everything you will ever need for your cat.

www.petsmart.com
Quality supplies and advice from this retail giant.

www.petstore.com
Good prices on food, toys, and whatever else you need.

www.petfooddirect.com
Good prices on all types of pet food.

SMP'S PET CARE BOOKS—
A PET OWNER'S BEST FRIEND . . .

Our books feature expert authors writing about today's most pressing pet care issues, from deciding to adopt to keeping a pet healthy.

ARE YOU THE PET FOR ME?
Choosing the Right Pet for Your Family
Mary Jane Checchi

WE'RE HAVING A KITTEN!
From the Big Decision Through the Crucial First Year
Eric Swanson

WE'RE HAVING A PUPPY!
From the Big Decision Through the Crucial First Year
Eric Swanson

AVAILABLE WHEREVER BOOKS ARE SOLD
FROM ST. MARTIN'S PAPERBACKS

The classic bestseller that began James
Herriot's extraordinary series...

All Creatures
Great and Small

JAMES HERRIOT

Let the world's most beloved animal doctor take
you along on his wonderful adventures through the
Yorkshire dales as he tends to its unforgettable
inhabitants—four-legged and otherwise.

"This warm, joyous and often hilarious first-person
chronicle of a young animal doctor...shines with
love of life."

—*The New York Times Book Review*

**AVAILABLE WHEREVER BOOKS ARE SOLD
FROM ST. MARTIN'S PAPERBACKS**

ALLC 3/98